GRE® CONTEXTUAL VOCABULARY

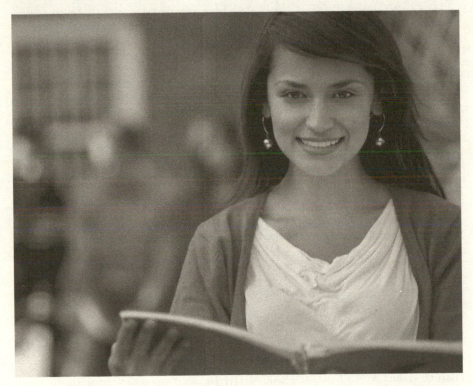

Ken Springer, Ph.D.

Department of Teaching and Learning
Southern Methodist University
Dallas, Texas

D0160986

Research & Education Association
Visit our website at: www.rea.com

Research & Education Association
61 Ethel Road West
Piscataway, New Jersey 08854
E-mail: info@rea.com

GRE® Contextual Vocabulary

Published 2013
Copyright © 2012 by Research & Education Association, Inc. All rights reserved. No part of this book may be reproduced in any form without permission of the publisher.

Printed in the United States of America

Library of Congress Control Number 2011932499

ISBN-13: 978-0-7386-0903-4
ISBN-10: 0-7386-0903-X

CONTENTS

Letter to the Student vi

About the Author vii

Overview: What This Book Is About viii

About Research & Education Association x

REA Acknowledgments xi

CHAPTER 1: Vocabulary Building 1: Exercises,
Activities, Games 1

    Unit 1 2

    Unit 2 5

    Review: Units 1 & 2 10

    Unit 3 14

    Unit 4 18

    Review: Units 3 & 4 22

    Unit 5 27

    Unit 6 31

    Review: Units 5 & 6 35

    Unit 7 40

    Unit 8 43

    Review: Units 7 & 8 49

    Unit 9 53

    Unit 10 59

    Review: Units 9 & 10 62

Unit 11 67
Unit 12 73
Review: Units 11 & 12 77

Answer Key: Chapter 1 83
Unit 1 83
Unit 2 85
Review: Units 1 & 2 88
Unit 3 91
Unit 4 93
Review: Units 3 & 4 96
Unit 5 99
Unit 6 101
Review: Units 5 & 6 104
Unit 7 108
Unit 8 110
Review: Units 7 & 8 112
Unit 9 115
Unit 10 117
Review: Units 9 & 10 120
Unit 11 123
Unit 12 125
Review: Units 11 & 12 128

CHAPTER 2: Vocabulary Building 2: Exercises,
Activities, Games 133
Unit 1 134
Unit 2 137
Review: Units 1 & 2 143
Unit 3 147
Unit 4 151
Review: Units 3 & 4 157
Unit 5 162
Unit 6 165
Review: Units 5 & 6 171
Unit 7 176

Unit 8 179
Review: Units 7 & 8 185
Unit 9 190
Unit 10 193
Review: Units 9 & 10 199
Unit 11 203
Unit 12 206
Review: Units 11 & 12 211

Answer Key: Chapter 2 216
Unit 1 216
Unit 2 218
Review: Units 1 & 2 221
Unit 3 224
Unit 4 226
Review: Units 3 & 4 229
Unit 5 232
Unit 6 234
Review: Units 5 & 6 238
Unit 7 242
Unit 8 244
Review: Units 7 & 8 248
Unit 9 251
Unit 10 253
Review: Units 9 & 10 257
Unit 11 260
Unit 12 262
Review: Units 11 & 12 265

CHAPTER 3: Vocabulary Building: Crossword Puzzles 269
Crossword Puzzle #1 270
Crossword Puzzle #2 272
Crossword Puzzle #3 274
Crossword Puzzle #4 276
Crossword Puzzle #5 278

Answers to Crossword Puzzles 280

Crossword Puzzle #1 280
Crossword Puzzle #2 281
Crossword Puzzle #3 282
Crossword Puzzle #4 283
Crossword Puzzle #5 284

CHAPTER 4: Vocabulary Building: Strategies and Resources 285
Expanding Your Vocabulary Horizons 286
Grammatical Cues 286

CHAPTER 5: GRE Verbal Reasoning: A Quick Introduction 291
Verbal Reasoning at a Glance 292
Examples of Question Types.................................... 292

CHAPTER 6: GRE Verbal Reasoning: Strategies for Success 297
General Strategies.. 298
Reading comprehension Stategies 299
Text completion Strategies...................................... 300
Sentence equivalence Strategies 302

Index of Key GRE Terms.. 305

Dear Student,

Although anyone can benefit from learning the vocabulary introduced in this book, you have most likely chosen the book because you plan to take the GRE and attend graduate or business school. Congratulations on pursuing this next step in your academic career!

As you know, performance on the GRE plays a critical role in the strength of applications to graduate and business programs. You may also know that beginning on August 1, 2011, the GRE General Test changed somewhat in form, content, and scoring. The test is now called the GRE revised General Test.

With respect to vocabulary, the Verbal Reasoning section of the GRE revised General Test places greater emphasis on higher-level cognitive skills. From the test taker's perspective, what this means is that the Verbal Reasoning section no longer contains questions that test vocabulary out of context. Antonyms and analogies have been dropped. As a result, all of the Verbal Reasoning questions now pertain to sentences or passages.

The revised Verbal Reasoning section is also distinctive in that it contains more reading comprehension questions, as well as new types of questions. All of these changes align the GRE revised General Test more closely with the academic expectations you will encounter in graduate or business school.

The three types of questions you will find in the revised Verbal Reasoning section are Reading Comprehension, Text Completion, and Sentence Equivalence.

Reading Comprehension questions appear in sets organized around passages. Some of these questions require you to select one answer choice out of five multiple-choice options. Others require you to choose one, two, or three answer choices out of three provided. A third type of Reading Comprehension question requires you to highlight a sentence in the passage that meets a certain description.

Text Completion questions consist of passages that contain one to three blanks. You are required to choose the word or words that best complete the passage.

Sentence Equivalence questions consist of a single sentence that contains a blank. You are required to choose two words from a list of six that would produce two sentences that are alike in meaning.

Detailed descriptions of these questions, as well as specific examples, are provided on the ETS website at: *www.ets.org/gre/revised_general/ about/content.*

Ken Springer, Ph.D.
Department of Teaching and Learning
Simmons School of Education and Human Development
Southern Methodist University

ABOUT THE AUTHOR

Dr. Ken Springer is a professor of education at Simmons School of Education and Human Development at Southern Methodist University. Dr. Springer is active in both teaching and research, with more than 60 scientific publications and presentations to his credit. Since 2010 he has authored or co-authored the following books: *Educational Research: A Contextual Approach* and *TExES: Generalist EC-6*. His recent work in English-language skill instruction includes co-authorship of REA's *CLEP College Composition Exams*, published in 2011.

OVERVIEW

What This Book Is About

This book is designed to improve your vocabulary. The focus is on the advanced vocabulary you will need for the GRE revised General Test. Having a well-developed vocabulary is useful in many settings and especially critical to successful performance on the GRE. In particular, the Verbal Reasoning section relies heavily on an understanding of advanced vocabulary. The quality of your responses to the Analytical Writing prompts depends in part on your knowing vocabulary that allows you to express your ideas clearly.

We use a contextual approach to teach new vocabulary. This approach does not rely on conventional flash-card methods. Rather, new words are introduced in meaningful contexts—i.e., in passages, most of which consist of brief narratives. Numerous exercises, activities, and puzzles are then provided in order to reinforce your understanding of the new words. Through this approach, learning new words should be fun rather than just being limited to the use of flash cards and drills.

Outline of the Book

The book consists of six chapters:

Chapters 1 and **2** provide context-based vocabulary instruction, along with exercises, activities, and games.

Chapter 3 consists of challenging crossword puzzles that test your understanding of what you learned in Chapters 1 and 2.

Chapter 4 introduces strategies and resources you can use to build your vocabulary further.

Chapter 5 presents a brief introduction to the GRE Verbal Reasoning section.

Chapter 6 describes strategies that will help you do your best on the GRE Verbal Reasoning section.

Guide to the First Two Chapters

Following is some information that will be helpful as you read Chapters 1 and 2—the chapters that provide instruction, and are the longest chapters in the book.

Chapters 1 and 2 consist of 12 units apiece. Each unit begins with a story in which advanced vocabulary words are underlined. You will be asked to guess the meanings of these words, and the meanings will then be provided. Next you will work through a series of exercises, activities, and games that reinforce and test your understanding of the new words. These exercises and so on consist of matching, fill-in-the-blanks, puzzles, and more.

In Chapters 1 and 2, every third unit will consist of a review that provides additional exercises, activities, and games that cover what you learned in the previous two units. Most of the review units will also introduce one or two new words. Answers to all of the exercises, activities, and games in the main units and review units are provided at the end of each chapter.

ABOUT RESEARCH & EDUCATION ASSOCIATION

Founded in 1959, Research & Education Association (REA) is dedicated to publishing the finest and most effective educational materials—including study guides and test preps—for students in middle school, high school, college, graduate school, and beyond.

Today, REA's wide-ranging catalog is a leading resource for teachers, students, and professionals. Visit *www.rea.com* to see a complete listing of all our titles.

REA ACKNOWLEDGMENTS

In addition to our authors, we would like to thank Pam Weston, Publisher, for setting the quality standards for production integrity and managing the publication to completion; Larry B. Kling, Vice President, Editorial, for his overall direction; Michael Reynolds, Managing Editor, for project management; Weymouth Design and Christine Saul, Senior Graphic Artist, for designing our cover; and S4Carlisle for typesetting this edition.

Overview

The purpose of this chapter is for you to learn new vocabulary. Much of this vocabulary has appeared in at least one prior version of the GRE Verbal Reasoning section.

The chapter consists of 12 units. Each unit begins with a section entitled "From inference to meaning" in which new words are introduced in meaningful contexts. Your knowledge of these new words is then reinforced through exercises, activities, and games. After every two units, you will also find a review section that goes back over the words you learned in those units. Answers to all activities are given in the Answer Key at the end of the chapter.

Unit 1

New words

Adversity	**Imminent**
Conciliate	**Reverberate**
Eminent	

From inference to meaning

Instructions: Read the following passage and use contextual information to guess the meanings of the underlined words. Then, have a look at the table below to see how accurately you guessed the meanings.

During his three years as a doctoral student, Jack had faced a number of challenges and setbacks. As a result, he was no stranger to adversity. His latest problem was that he had forgotten to complete an assignment for his advisor, Dr. Rik Ingrid, an eminent scholar whose fame was accompanied by a nasty temper. As he stood in the doorway of Dr. Ingrid's office, trying to explain why the assignment wasn't ready, Jack knew that a stormy reaction was imminent. Although he tried to conciliate Dr. Ingrid, Jack's girlfriend told him later that she had heard his advisor's loudly delivered criticism reverberate all the way down the hall.

Your guesses

Adversity: _____   **Imminent:** _____

Conciliate: _____   **Reverberate:** _____

Eminent: _____

Definitions

Adversity: difficulty

Conciliate: pacify; make calm

Eminent: famous; prominent

Imminent: about to happen

Reverberate: echo

■ Word fuse

Instructions: Draw a line between each fragment in the left column and one fragment in the right column to create a word.

IM	VERSITY
CON	INENT
RE	VERBERATE
EM	CILIATE
AD	MINENT

■ Fill-ins

Instructions: Fill in the blank in each sentence below with one of the words from the following list:

adversity   conciliate   eminent   imminent   reverberate

1. Once the thunder and lightning started, we knew that rain was _____.

2. It is easier to aggravate a person than it is to _____ him or her.

3. His was a life filled with _____, having spent time in jail on three separate occasions, and then finding it difficult to convince employers to hire him.

4. Sheronica could hear the sound of the engine _____ in the cool autumn air.

5. Who do you consider the most _____ researcher in the field of genetic engineering?

■ Word scramble

Instructions: Unscramble each of the following words. Use the hints below as needed.

1) R D T V Y S A E I _____

2) E I T N M N I M _____

3) I C T L A O N I C E _____

4) E B V A R R E E E T R _____

5) T N I E N M E _____

Hints:
1) difficulty, 2) about to happen, 3) pacify, 4) echo, 5) famous

■ Matching

Instructions: Draw a line between words that have the same meaning.

echo   famous

eminent   conciliate

pacify   difficulty

about to happen   reverberate

adversity   imminent

■ Unit 2

New words

Abate   Gingerly
Apotheosis   Insensible
Assuage   Jovially
Descry   Vying

■ From inference to meaning

Instructions: Read the following passage and use contextual information to guess the meanings of the underlined words. Then, have a look at the table below to see how accurately you guessed the meanings.

Stunned by a nearby explosion, the young soldier lay on the ground without moving, almost <u>insensible</u> owing to the force of the blast. Then he looked up. Through the smoke he could just barely <u>descry</u> a staff sergeant, the leader of his squad, walking toward him from a small building. This particular staff sergeant was the <u>apotheosis</u> of courage. In battle he was resolute, and he often risked his own safety to help the men under his command. Watching this brave man approach, the wounded soldier felt a sense of relief, and the anxiety that had been gripping him began to abate. "Nice day," said the staff sergeant jovially when he reached the soldier, "Any plans for the evening?" The sergeant was making a little joke, of course, trying to assuage the young man's fear. "Not sure yet," replied the soldier, vying with the sergeant to see who could be funnier, "know of any good movies?" The sergeant laughed. "Come on," he said, and with that he helped the soldier to his feet as gingerly as possible and guided him quickly to safety.

Your guesses

Abate: _____   Gingerly: _____

Apotheosis: _____   Insensible: _____

Assuage: _____   Jovially: _____

Descry: _____   Vying: _____

Definitions

Abate: become less; diminish   **Gingerly:** carefully; delicately

Apotheosis: ideal model   **Insensible:** unresponsive

Assuage: soothe   **Jovially:** in a jolly way

Descry: catch sight of   **Vying:** competing with

■ Word fuse

Instructions: Draw a line between each fragment in the left column and one fragment in the right column to create a word.

DES	SIBLE
JOVI	ATE
INSEN	THEOSIS
APO	CRY
VYI	NG
GIN	SUAGE
AB	ALLY
AS	GERLY

■ Fill-ins

Instructions: Fill in the blank in each sentence below with one of the words from the following list:

abate	apotheosis	assuage	descry
gingerly	insensible	jovially	vying

1. With a big smile and a warm hug, my uncle greeted me _____.

2. Linda wasn't able to _____ her father's concerns about her recent car trouble.

3. Although the grass beside the lake was tall and dense, the hunter believed that while hiding there he would still be able to _____ the ducks as they landed on the water.

4. With her straight-A average and her prowess on the soccer field, Mary is the _____ of the scholar-athlete.

5. The effects of the illness rendered the young man almost completely _____.

6. After injuring my foot, I had to walk very _____.

7. Two hours into the spelling bee, there were still four contestants _____ for the championship.

8. Instead of taking a pain reliever, Carlos simply waited for the pain from his headache to _____.

▋ Word scramble

Instructions: Unscramble each of the following words. Use the hints below as needed.

1) E E I N B N L S S I _____

2) Y V N G I _____

3) A E T A B _____

4) R I E G Y N L G _____

5) S H P O E A I S O T _____

6) I L O Y V L A J _____

7) E R Y D C S _____

8) U S G S A E A _____

Hints:
1) unresponsive, 2) competing with, 3) become less, 4) carefully, 5) ideal model,
6) in a jolly way, 7) catch sight of, 8) soothe

■ Matching

Instructions: Draw a line between words that have the same meaning.

competing with	apotheosis
jovially	unresponsive
gingerly	vying
ideal model	abate
insensible	assuage
become less	carefully
descry	in a jolly way
soothe	catch sight of

Review: Units 1 & 2

Contrasts

Key vocabulary words may be confused with each other because they differ in just one sound. For example, consider the adjectives "eminent" and "imminent." "Eminent" is usually used to describe a person. Although not common, you can also describe an object as eminent (e.g., a person can speak of an eminent peak). "Imminent" is used to describe events. An imminent event is one that is about to happen (e.g., a person can speak of an imminent threat). Here are some examples:

1. The islanders were unsure whether the volcano on their island was about to erupt, so they hired an *eminent* authority to conduct an investigation. Following the investigation, the authority warned the islanders that an eruption was *imminent*.

2. Because of his long and dedicated career of public service, our mayor has become an *eminent* politician. Many observers feel that a run for the office of governor is *imminent*.

Fast facts

1. The verb "descry" has two meanings: It can mean "catch sight of," as in the passage in Unit 2. Alternatively, it can mean "proclaim" (e.g., "He wandered through the village attempting to descry the strength of the coming storm.").

2. The word "conciliate" comes from a Latin word meaning "bring together"—the same Latin word that forms the basis of "reconcile." The prefix "con" means "together." You can see how this prefix functions in words such as *connect*, *construct*, and *convene*. As an adjective, "consonant" means "being in agreement." For example:

Justine had been upset that Braylen appeared to disagree with her; later, she was *conciliated* by the realization that Braylen's views were actually *consonant* with her own.

■ Grammar stretches

Instructions: Fill in the blank in each sentence below with one of the words from the following list. You may have to change the grammatical form of each word in order for it to fit into a sentence.

abate adversity apotheosis assuage conciliate descry
eminent imminent insensible jovially reverberate vying

1. As the race progressed, the two American runners began to
   _____ for the lead.

2. Wherever he worked, the doctor had a profound influence on his colleagues because of his _____ in the field of medicine.

3. Although Mr. Jackson was worried, he attempted to be _____
   so that his colleagues at the meeting wouldn't think there was a problem.

4. I consider these two scientists to be _____ of professional
   commitment.

5. On the morning after the concert, Efrain woke up with the sounds of
   electric guitars still _____ in his head.

6. She has the capacity to succeed no matter how _____ her
   circumstances.

7. What concerns me most about the economic downturn she predicted
   for next month is not its magnitude but rather its _____.

8. Long after the flooding had _____, the citizens continued
   to deal with the aftermath of the storm.

9. Rather than adopting a _____ attitude, Rosemary met her
   critic's hostility with some angry words of her own.

10. I spoke as reassuringly as I could, but I'm not sure whether I
_____ her fears.

11. The soldiers watched the sky carefully until they had
_____ a plane.

12. As the man became more intoxicated and unable to comprehend
what we were telling him, he began to speak more and more
_____.

■ Error watch

Instructions: In the following sentences, note whether the underlined word is used correctly or not. Circle the C at the end of the sentence if the word is used correctly; circle the I if it is used incorrectly.

1. Even if she holds her son's hand during a visit to the dentist, she is unable to <u>descry</u> his fear.   C   I

2. When the plumber banged on the pipes, a clanging sound <u>reverberated</u> all around the building.   C   I

3. People all over the world recognized this <u>imminent</u> actor whenever he made an appearance.   C   I

4. Due to his inexperience, the employee didn't know how to <u>abate</u> the angry customer.   C   I

5. Emilio grew up in a loving, happy, and rather sheltered environment; as a result, he considered himself fairly inexperienced at dealing with <u>adversity</u>.   C   I

6. Abraham Lincoln is one of America's most <u>apotheosis</u> political figures.   C   I

■ Matching

Instructions: Draw a line between words that have the same meaning.

vying	catch sight of
ideal model	become less
adversity	competing with
descry	in a jolly way
about to happen	echo
reverberate	soothe
carefully	apotheosis
eminent	insensible
pacify	difficulty
abate	imminent
unresponsive	conciliate
assuage	gingerly
jovially	famous

Unit 3

New words

Berate	Intransigent
Derogatory	Preclude
Embroiled	Rejoinder
Impugn	Tirade

From inference to meaning

Instructions: Read the following passage and use contextual information to guess the meanings of the underlined words. Then, have a look at the table below to see how accurately you guessed the meanings.

During the flight, Jay could tell that the couple seated next to him would soon be underlined embroiled in an argument. First the man made a derogatory remark about the woman's clothing, accusing her of looking cheap. The woman's curt rejoinder was that her intent was to wear something comfortable, not stylish. The man fell silent for a moment. Then he began to impugn the woman's logic, arguing that being comfortable doesn't preclude dressing well. The woman replied that the man himself was wearing rather old and scruffy shoes. Upon hearing this, the man launched into a tirade, pausing only to lean in closer to the woman so that others on the plane would not hear his angry words. The woman asked him to stop talking, or at least to change the subject, but the man was intransigent and continued to berate her.

Your guesses

Berate: _____	Intransigent: _____
Derogatory: _____	Preclude: _____
Embroiled: _____	Rejoinder: _____
Impugn: _____	Tirade: _____

Definitions

Berate: scold angrily

Derogatory: insulting

Embroiled: deeply involved; entangled

Impugn: verbally attack

Intransigent: unwilling to compromise

Preclude: rule out; prevent

Rejoinder: quick reply

Tirade: long, angry speech

▮ Word fuse

Instructions: Draw a line between each fragment in the left column and one fragment in the right column to create a word.

TI	SIGENT
RE	GATORY
INTRAN	PUGN
DERO	RADE
PRE	BROILED
BER	CLUDE
EM	JOINDER
IM	ATE

■ Fill-ins

Instructions: Fill in the blank in each sentence below with one of the words from the following list:

berate	derogatory	embroiled	impugn
intransigent	preclude	rejoinder	tirade

1. We argued for two hours but neither one of us could convince the other one of anything; I guess we were both pretty _____.

2. As Flannery O'Connor once said, "Accepting oneself does not _____ an attempt to become better."

3. He was hurt by her remarks because they were not just critical but also _____.

4. The speaker's comments were clearly intended to _____ the reputation of the congresswoman.

5. Marta made a witty comment about John's awful haircut, but John was unable to come up with a good _____.

6. If you have a complaint, feel free to speak to me, but please do not _____ me.

7. At the end of his _____, I was worn out by the length as well as the underlying hostility of his comments.

8. For years the two neighbors had been _____ in a largely friendly but complicated disagreement over the boundaries of their property lines.

Word scramble

Instructions: Unscramble each of the following words. Use the hints below as needed.

1) U C P E L D E R _____

2) D M B E O L E R I _____

3) T O A R O G E Y R D _____

4) G U M I N P _____

5) N O R J R D I E E _____

6) R E D I T A _____

7) T B A E E R _____

8) E I T T A I N N N S G R _____

Hints:
1) rule out, 2) deeply involved, 3) insulting, 4) verbally attack, 5) quick reply,
6) long, angry speech, 7) scold angrily, 8) unwilling to compromise

■ Matching

Instructions: Draw a line between words that have the same meaning.

deeply involved	long, angry speech
impugn	rejoinder
rule out	unwilling to compromise
quick reply	embroiled
intransigent	derogatory
insulting	berate
tirade	verbally attack
scold angrily	preclude

■ Unit 4

New words

Discern	**Prone**
Incisively	**Resolute**
Morass	

■ From inference to meaning

Instructions: Read the following excerpt from Dr. Martin Luther King Jr.'s speech "The Purpose of Education" and guess the meanings of the underlined words. Then, have a look at the table below to see how accurately you guessed the meanings.

Education must also train one for quick, <u>resolute</u> and effective thinking. To think <u>incisively</u> and to think for one's self is very difficult. We are <u>prone</u> to let our mental life become invaded by legions of half-truths, prejudices, and propaganda...To save man from the <u>morass</u> of propaganda, in my opinion, is one of the chief aims of education. Education must enable one to sift and weigh evidence, to <u>discern</u> the true from the false, the real from the unreal, and the facts from the fiction.

Your guesses

Discern: _____   Prone: _____

Incisively: _____   Resolute: _____

Morass: _____

Definitions

Discern: perceive; distinguish   **Prone:** likely to

Incisively: analytically; intelligently   **Resolute:** determined; unhesitating

Morass: swamp; complicated, confusing or troublesome situation

Word fuse

Instructions: Draw a line between each fragment in the left column and one fragment in the right column to create a word.

MO	SIVELY
DIS	NE
RESO	RASS
PRO	LUTE
INCI	CERN

Fill-ins

Instructions: Fill in the blank in each sentence below with one of the words from the following list:

discern   incisively   morass   prone   resolute

1. She was _____ to experiencing headaches whenever her level of stress was high.

2. Because of the fog, the pilot was unable to _____ whether the lights up ahead were from a runway.

3. Due to the abrupt resignation of the prime minister and more than half of his cabinet, the political situation in the country had become a _____.

4. The critic spoke _____ about the limitations of recent attempts to understand Shakespeare through computer analysis.

5. In private, the congresswoman seemed uncertain about how to address the budget crisis, but once the cameras were rolling she became more _____.

■ Word scramble

Instructions: Unscramble each of the following words. Use the hints below as needed.

1) T R S L E E O U _____

2) R I S N C E D _____

3) R E N P O _____

4) N V E C I Y S I I L _____

5) A M R S S O _____

Hints:
1) determined, 2) perceive, 3) likely to, 4) analytically, 5) swamp

■ Matching

Instructions: Draw a line between words that have the same meaning.

likely to	swamp
morass	prone
determined	discern
incisively	analytically
perceive	resolute

Review: Units 3 & 4

Contrasts

1. The words "intransigent" and "resolute" are similar in meaning, in that both can be used to refer to a person who is unyielding. At the same time, "intransigent" conveys a more negative impression. An intransigent person is one who responds to conflict by stubbornly refusing to compromise. A resolute person is simply firm in his or her beliefs or actions. For example:

   "In any political discussion he was intransigent and refused to consider alternative perspectives."

   "She was resolute in her faith that democracy would prevail."

2. The words "berate" and "impugn" are similar in meaning, in that both imply a verbal attack. However, "berate" is often use to describe the action of complaining or expressing anger against someone. In other words, one berates a person. "Impugn" is often used to describe the action of criticizing a person's ideas or reputation. For example:

   "She berated him for his mistake."

   "He impugned her favorite beliefs."

Fast facts

1. The verb "impugn" comes from the Latin words "in" (upon) and "pugnare" (to fight). Currently "impugn" does not refer to fighting in general, but rather to a verbal attack on an idea or person. However, you can see how the word is related to its Latin roots. You can also see how the verb "pugnare" is used in a similar way in other English words. For example, a "pugnacious" person is one who tends to be hostile and aggressive. A "pugilist" is someone who fights with the fists (i.e., a boxer). For example:

   It is risky to *impugn* the reputation of a *pugilist*, especially if he is *pugnacious*.

2. The word "prone" comes from the Latin "pronus," which has a concrete sense ("bent forward") as well as a more abstract sense ("likely to"). As an adjective, "prone" is used in the abstract sense to mean "likely to." The abstract sense and the concrete sense are related. A person who is prone to think or act a certain way is, so to speak, bending toward that thought or action. As an adjective, "prone" can be also used in a purely concrete sense to refer to someone or something in a downward-facing position. A person who is lying face down can be described as prone, or lying in a prone position. To "pronate" means to turn the palm face down, and when describing a running person, "pronation" refers to an inward and downward movement of the foot as it contacts the ground. For example:

Teddy's *pronation* was so severe that he was *prone* to stumbling whenever he ran too fast.

■ Fill-ins

Instructions: Fill in the blank in each sentence below with one of the words from the following list:

derogatory   morass   preclude   prone   resolute   tirade

1. Working full-time and raising a family do not necessarily _____ taking care of oneself.

2. The waiter was offended by the _____ comments that the diner kept making about his lunch.

3. If you say anything to him about the economy, Darius is likely to respond with a _____ against the business practices of multinational corporations.

4. What a _____ this problem has become!

5. This particular district is _____ to relatively dramatic shifts in voting preferences from election to election.

6. In spite of numerous obstacles, the teacher was _____ in her belief that this would be a good year for her students.

■ Grammar stretches

Instructions: Fill in the blank in each sentence below with one of the words from the following list. You may have to change the grammatical form of each word in order for it to fit into a sentence.

berate	discern	embroiled	impugn
incisively	intransigent	rejoinder	

1. If you keep on _____ his reputation, he is likely to become offended.

2. No matter how often the comedian was heckled by an audience member, she always had witty _____.

3. The debater was brilliant and _____ about the need for grass-roots educational reform.

4. Because he lacked the capacity for _____, he often chose the wrong people to associate with.

5. The two archeologists were slowly _____ me in their complicated dispute about who had been first to identify the lost settlement.

6. Mr. White showed so much hostility and _____ in his refusal to consider our counteroffer.

7. It bothered Jasmine that the young mother had _____ her young son for spilling the milk.

■ Error watch

Instructions: In the following sentences, note whether the underlined word is used correctly or not. Circle the C at the end of the sentence if the word is used correctly; circle the I if it is used incorrectly.

1. No matter what I said, he refused to change his mind. He was so <u>discerning</u>!   C   I

2. Being healthy does not <u>preclude</u> the possibility of developing diabetes when one gets older.   C   I

3. I felt very <u>impugned</u> in this situation, because it demanded so much of my time and energy.   C   I

4. She is very <u>resolute</u> about her plan to apply to graduate school.   C   I

5. <u>Intransigence</u> will not help you get what you want from him; you need to be more cooperative.   C   I

■ Matching

Instructions: Draw a line between words that have the same meaning.

preclude	unwilling to compromise
swamp	prone
deeply involved	long, angry speech
incisively	rule out
intransigent	derogatory
insulting	berate
scold angrily	analytically
quick reply	discern
tirade	resolute
distinguish	verbally attack
likely to	morass
impugn	rejoinder
determined	embroiled

Unit 5

From inference to meaning

Instructions: Read the following passage and use contextual information to guess the meanings of the underlined words. Then, have a look at the table below to see how accurately you guessed the meanings.

Winding its way around the mountain, the road became increasingly <u>perilous</u>, and so I asked the cab driver to slow down. Although he had been <u>taciturn</u> throughout most of the trip, the driver saw now that I was afraid, and so he began to chat with me, shifting from topic to topic in a much-appreciated attempt to <u>alleviate</u> my fears. It turned out that he was a <u>querulous</u> man, full of complaints about the government, the cab company that employed him, his mother-in-law, his two sons, and almost any other topic that he discussed. The more he talked, the more I realized that he was exceedingly <u>garrulous</u> too—a natural talker—but that in spite of the querulous nature of his comments, he was basically <u>gregarious</u> and enjoyed interacting with people. Unfortunately, he seemed to enjoy talking more than listening, and after a few attempts to hold up my end of the conversation I realized that my efforts were <u>futile</u>. I gave up, leaned back in my seat, and let his monologue <u>saturate</u> the warm air of the cab.

Your guesses

Alleviate: _____   Perilous: _____

Futile: _____   Querulous: _____

Garrulous: _____   Saturate: _____

Gregarious: _____   Taciturn: _____

Definitions

Alleviate: relieve; make easier

Futile: ineffective; useless

Garrulous: overly talkative

Gregarious: sociable

Perilous: dangerous

Querulous: often complaining

Saturate: completely fill; soak

Taciturn: not talkative; reserved

Word fuse

Instructions: Draw a line between each fragment in the left column and one fragment in the right column to create a word.

PERI	IATE
FUT	ARIOUS
QUER	RULOUS
GREG	URATE
TACI	TURN
SAT	LOUS
ALLEV	ULOUS
GAR	ILE

■ Fill-ins

Instructions: Fill in the blank in each sentence below with one of the words from the following list:

alleviate	futile	garrulous	gregarious
perilous	querulous	saturate	taciturn

1. Due to his _____ nature, Juan found fault will all of the solutions I proposed for his computer problem.

2. Attempting to walk across a busy freeway at night is _____, no matter how carefully one proceeds.

3. As he scrubbed the wall, Kevin realized that any attempts to prevent tiny chips of paint from flaking off would be _____.

4. The eyewitness did not provide many details about the crime, in part because she was so _____.

5. Although ordinarily a man of few words, Quinton became quite _____ once he began discussing a topic that interested him.

6. The moment she walked into the room, her perfume began to _____ the air.

7. The aspirin that Ling took failed to _____ the pain from her knee injury.

8. Because Johannes is so_____, he seeks a job in which he would have many opportunities to interact with people.

■ Word scramble

Instructions: Unscramble each of the following words. Use the hints below as needed.

1) U A R S R L O G U _____

2) T E R U A A S T _____

3) U L E P I O S R _____

4) L T I E E I V A L _____

5) U E R S O U U L Q _____

6) E U R R S I A O G G _____

7) T N R T I U A C _____

8) U L I F E T _____

Hints:
1) overly talkative, 2) completely fill, 3) dangerous, 4) relieve, 5) often complaining,
6) sociable, 7) not talkative, 8) ineffective

Matching

Instructions: Draw a line between words that have the same meaning.

not talkative	relieve
querulous	gregarious
perilous	ineffective
alleviate	dangerous
completely fill	saturate
sociable	often complaining
overly talkative	taciturn
futile	garrulous

Unit 6

New words

Besotted	Lacerate
Epitaph	Liberty
Indignation	

From inference to meaning

Instructions: The following poem was written by W. B. Yeats in honor of the previously deceased writer Jonathan Swift. Read the poem and use contextual information to guess the meanings of the underlined words. Then, have a look at the table below to see how accurately you guessed the meanings.

"Swift's <u>Epitaph</u>"

Swift has sailed into his rest;

Savage <u>indignation</u> there

Cannot <u>lacerate</u> his Breast.

Imitate him if you dare,

World-<u>Besotted</u> Traveler; he

Served human <u>liberty</u>.

Your guesses

Besotted: _____   Lacerate: _____

Epitaph: _____   Liberty: _____

Indignation: _____

Definitions

Besotted: intoxicated; infatuated

Epitaph: commemorative text on tombstone or monument

Indignation: anger over injustice

Lacerate: cut irregularly; slash

Liberty: freedom

Word fuse

Instructions: Draw a line between each fragment in the left column and one fragment in the right column to create a word.

LAC   NATION

INDIG   TAPH

LIBE   ERATE

EPI   TTED

BESO   RTY

Fill-ins

Instructions: Fill in the blank in each sentence below with one of the words from the following list:

besotted   epitaph   indignation   lacerate   liberty

1. Because they felt that the mayor had been dishonest, the city council addressed him with considerable _____.

2. Freedom of speech does not give citizens the _____ to say anything they want to say in every possible situation.

3. The _____ on the gravestone indicated that Smith had been a prominent social activist in her day.

4. After spending most of the day relaxing at the beach and drinking margaritas, the man was so _____ with alcohol and sun he could barely find the way back to his hotel room.

5. The stunt man took precautions so that he would not _____ his skin when he leapt through the plate glass window.

■ Word scramble

Instructions: Unscramble each of the following words. Use the hints below as needed.

1) Y L R I T B E _____

2) P P E I T H A _____

3) E A C A E R L T _____

4) S B D T E T O E _____

5) I I N O D G T I A N N _____

Hints:
1) freedom, 2) commemorative text, 3) cut irregularly, 4) intoxicated, 5) anger

■ Matching

Instructions: Draw a line between words that have the same meaning.

cut irregularly   commemorative text

indignation   freedom

epitaph   besotted

liberty   lacerate

intoxicated   anger

Review: Units 5 & 6

Contrasts

1. The verbs "conciliate" (see Unit 1), "alleviate," and "assuage" (Unit 2) all refer to the reduction of unpleasantness. However, "conciliate" pertains to the reduction of unpleasantness arising from conflict, as when a person conciliates another person who has had to yield a point in an argument. "Alleviate" and "assuage" refer more generally to the reduction of pain or emotional distress in any situation, not just one in which there is conflict. "Alleviate" in particular suggests that the reduction of pain is partial or temporary, as when medicine is taken to alleviate the symptoms of an illness. For example:

   Bryson and Rachel argued for almost ten minutes before David decided to add some *conciliatory* remarks to the conversation. Speaking cautiously, David managed to *alleviate* some of the tension that had arisen. However, he knew that he would have to speak to each of his friends separately in order to fully *assuage* their concerns.

2. The adjectives "garrulous" and "taciturn" are antonyms.

Fast facts

1. The word "indignation" is a combination of the Latin words "in" (not) and "dignus" (worthy). "Indignation" does not currently mean "unworthy." Rather, a sense of indignation means that someone feels anger at some person or situation that is unworthy of greater esteem—because the person has acted wrongly, or the situation is unjust. In other English words, the Latin root "dignus" more directly conveys a sense of worth, as in the words "dignified" and "dignity." In addition, the word "deign," which means "to consider worthy," can also be traced to the same origin.

2. The verb "liberty" comes from "liber," the Latin word for "freedom." There are several English words related to freedom that trace their origins to this Latin root. Examples include "liberate"

and "liberal." A "libertine" is a person who is largely free of morals. For example:

> After Stephan got drunk and described how much he enjoys shop-lifting, I realized that he is not just a *liberal* person—he's a *libertine*.

▮ Grammar stretches

Instructions: Fill in the blank in each sentence below with one of the words from the following list. You may have to change the grammatical form of each word in order for it to fit into a sentence.

alleviate	epitaph	futile	garrulous	gregarious
indignation	lacerate	perilous	querulous	saturate

1. Larry was _____ at the suggestion that he had not tried his hardest during the team's last game.

2. Juanita's natural _____ makes her a delightful addition to any dinner party.

3. Once the cotton ball was completely _____ with alcohol, I dabbed the wound carefully.

4. He avoided skydiving because of the inherent _____ of the activity.

5. Although the chair of the meeting asked Krystal to be brief, she addressed us most _____.

6. He finds that a hot bath goes a long way toward _____ the stress of a long day's work.

7. As a result of the accident, Jace had _____ on both hands and forearms.

8. One could not possibly read all of the _____ at Arlington National Cemetery.

9. There is no way John could ever be a congressman; the time he spends thinking about a congressional bid is an exercise in _____.

10. Talking to Jini always tried my patience due to the _____ of her comments about her family and friends.

▪ Error watch

Instructions: In the following sentences, note whether the underlined word is used correctly or not. Circle the C at the end of the sentence if the word is used correctly; circle the I if it is used incorrectly.

1. After the waiter spilled a glass of water on him, Micah's shirt was almost completely <u>saturated</u>.   C   I

2. "You always complain when things don't go your way. I wish you were less <u>garrulous</u>!"   C   I

3. The public expressed a great deal of <u>alleviation</u> over the judge's mishandling of the case.   C   I

4. The Secret Service agent was not at <u>liberty</u> to discuss her current activities.   C   I

5. During their relationship, Keisha felt that Joe rarely expressed himself as much as he should have; she often wished that he would be more <u>taciturn</u>.   C   I

6. The bumblebee flew in a crooked path from flower to flower as if it were <u>besotted</u> with nectar.   C   I

7. Because of the civil war, it is <u>perilous</u> to visit the country at the present time.   C   I

8. Because he is so <u>futile</u>, it is difficult to get him to change his thinking.   C   I

▪ Matching

Instructions: Draw a line between words that have the same meaning.

futile	garrulous
relieve	anger
cut irregularly	besotted
indignation	liberty
overly talkative	alleviate
epitaph	saturate
freedom	commemorative text
taciturn	lacerate
querulous	sociable
perilous	ineffective
intoxicated	dangerous
completely fill	not talkative
gregarious	often complaining

■ Word Search

Instructions: All of the new words from Units 5 and 6 are hidden in this challenging puzzle. The words may be written forwards or backwards in any direction: horizontal, vertical, or diagonal. Some words overlap in one letter. Your task is to circle each word as you have found it.

Following are the meanings of the words you're looking for. (Remember: You're searching for the actual words, not the meanings given here.)

overly talkative	completely fill	dangerous	relieve
often complaining	sociable	not talkative	ineffective freedom
commemorative text	cut irregularly	intoxicated	anger

```
A L I N A H P F I C T P E T E V I E O D
L T E R E O D E G R E G A R I O U S L A
L O E E M N F U N E S P T O A N D E M R
T M S U O L U R R A G E I S E G E D U S
O U I C H T T L A S W R N T R B T E L H
E Y K J A Y I O N H Q O T E A R I R I A
F T E L S O L A Y N U V I A G P O D B S
B E S O T T E D R O F U S S E U H R E T
R V L R N R E O O N I L N O K L O E R O
N E I Z E S B R X C R C A L H B A U T S
O X T L F E I S A H T U W I E O L Y Y U
E S C A S J G I Y E E N T N O D I R J O
W U E C D H I N A I R G O I G E F H O L
D O I E M O D U P P E E H E C D S E M U
A L A R S N B C O A D R A Q U A T A L R
S I L A U E T I O N S A T U R A T E I E
F R I T N E P T D I N M E T W M O M E U
G E L E T O S A Y T U R N U T O W E O Q
E P I N I E B R A L E C U L E L B R A R
R E E R O A N I N D I G N A T I O N Y I
E A R T O L K S W E E D C F A R E L N L
E M A L O K E N I Y E F O E L I T E G E
A L L E V I A T E W A R I N A E M T S U
M A L G E O U R L O I G D E N I R E U Q
```

Unit 7

New words

Pecuniary

Soporific

Stolidity

Torpor

Whimsical

From inference to meaning

Instructions: Read the following passage and use contextual information to guess the meanings of the underlined words. Then, have a look at the table below to see how accurately you guessed the meanings.

Professor Mathers was an extraordinarily serious man. Those who knew him well suspected that he had never experienced a whimsical moment in his entire life, even as a child. The professor was an economist whose expertise included personal finance—he was an expert on pecuniary matters. Naturally, if you were to approach the professor with a question about financial planning, his stolidity would be much appreciated. One does not hope for drama and passion in the advice one receives about money. However, if you were a student attending one of his lectures, the professor's dry approach was utterly soporific, and you would soon find yourself nodding off. Professor Mathers had a knack for reducing an entire classroom of eager students to a state of complete torpor.

Your guesses

Pecuniary: _____

Soporific: _____

Stolidity: _____

Torpor: _____

Whimsical: _____

Definitions

Pecuniary: monetary; related to money

Soporific: sleep-producing

Stolidity: emotionlessness

Torpor: listlessness; inactivity

Whimsical: playful; impulsive

Word fuse

Instructions: Draw a line between each fragment in the left column and one fragment in the right column to create a word.

WHIM	DITY
STOLI	IFIC
TOR	IARY
PECUN	SICAL
SOPOR	POR

Fill-ins

Instructions: Fill in the blank in each sentence below with one of the words from the following list:

pecuniary   soporific   stolidity   torpor   whimsical

1. Reading late at night has a _____ effect on some people, as it helps them fall right to sleep.

2. Karima's sudden decision to paint her room lavender was one of her more _____ ideas.

3. When the ship grazed the iceberg, the captain's _____ helped keep the crew from becoming overly panicked.

4. The musician was so late to his own concert that a general _____ had settled over the audience well before he took the stage.

5. As a corporate attorney, one of her responsibilities was to protect her company's _____ interests.

◼ Word scramble

Instructions: Unscramble each of the following words. Use the hints below as needed.

1) C R O I P F O I S _____

2) R R O O P T _____

3) C I W L H S M A I _____

4) E C Y P U I R A N _____

5) Y T S T I O I L D _____

Hints:
1) sleep-producing, 2) listlessness, 3) playful, 4) monetary, 5) emotionlessness

■ Matching

Instructions: Draw a line between words that have the same meaning.

emotionlessness	monetary
pecuniary	sleep-producing
playful	torpor
listlessness	whimsical
soporific	stolidity

■ Unit 8

New words

Chastisement	Inclined
Counterpart	Jocosely
Eccentricity	Reverent
Hereditary	

■ From inference to meaning

Instructions: Read the following excerpt from Mark Twain's "A New Crime" and guess the meanings of the underlined words. Then, have a look at the table below to see how accurately you guessed the meanings.

Take the case of Lynch Hackett, of Pennsylvania. Twice, in public, he attacked a German butcher by the name of Bemis Feldner, with a cane, and both times Feldner whipped him with his fists. Hackett was a vain, wealthy, violent gentleman, who held his blood and family in high esteem, and believed that a <u>reverent</u> respect was due to his great riches. He brooded over the shame of his <u>chastisement</u> for two weeks, and then, in a momentary fit of insanity, armed himself to the teeth, rode into town, waited a couple of hours until he saw Feldner coming down the street with his wife on his arm, and then, as the couple passed the doorway in which he had partially concealed himself, he drove a knife into Feldner's neck, killing him instantly. The widow caught the limp form and eased it to the earth. Both were drenched with blood. Hackett <u>jocosely</u> remarked to her that as a professional butcher's recent wife she could appreciate the artistic neatness of the job that left her in condition to marry again, in case she wanted to. This remark, and another which he made to a friend, that his position in society made the killing of an obscure citizen simply an "<u>eccentricity</u>" instead of a crime, were shown to be evidences of insanity, and so Hackett escaped punishment. The jury were hardly <u>inclined</u> to accept these as proofs at first, inasmuch as the prisoner had never been insane before the murder, and under the tranquilizing effect of the butchering had immediately regained his right mind; but when the defense came to show that a third cousin of Hackett's wife's step-father was insane, and not only insane, but had a nose the very <u>counterpart</u> of Hackett's, it was plain that insanity was <u>hereditary</u> in the family, and Hackett had come by it by legitimate inheritance. Of course the jury then acquitted him...

Your guesses

Chastisement: _____   Inclined: _____

Counterpart: _____   Jocosely: _____

Eccentricity: _____   Reverent: _____

Hereditary: _____

Definitions

Chastisement: punishment; scolding

Counterpart: thing that resembles, duplicates, or complements another

Eccentricity: unconventional behavior

Hereditary: inherited; ancestral

Inclined: likely; having a preference

Jocosely: with humor

Reverent: deeply respectful

Word fuse

Instructions: Draw a line between each fragment in the left column and one fragment in the right column to create a word.

JOC	ERENT
ECCEN	TERPART
REV	LINED
COUN	OSELY
HERED	TISEMENT
CHAS	TRICITY
INC	ITARY

Fill-ins

Instructions: Fill in the blank in each sentence below with one of the words from the following list:

chastisement   counterpart   eccentricity   hereditary
inclined   jocosely   reverent

1. I work hard for my money, and so I'm not _____ to spend it freely.

2. Nia's most noticeable _____ is her choice of hair color—orange on one side of her head, blue on the other.

3. Having studied and written about the visual arts for many years, Dwayne had a _____ attitude toward geniuses such as Picasso.

4. I suspect that the vice president in my company makes very little money as compared to her _____ in your company.

5. Melanie's hearing loss was not due to accident or illness; rather, it was _____.

6. His crimes call for more _____ than I have the energy to deliver.

7. Though the recent firings were a serious matter, the employees in Wilma's unit treated the topic of their job security _____.

■ Word scramble

Instructions: Unscramble each of the following words. Use the hints below as needed.

1) T Y H D R E R E A I _____

2) T E E E V N R R _____

3) O E L J C Y O S _____

4) C E N I A M E S T H S T _____

5) R E C T C E T Y C I I N _____

6) D I I N C N E L _____

7) T E T U O P C N R R A _____

Hints:
1) inherited, 2) deeply respectful, 3) with humor, 4) punishment, 5) unconventional behavior, 6) likely, 7) thing that resembles another

■ Matching

Instructions: Draw a line between words that have the same meaning.

inherited	inclined
reverent	with humor
eccentricity	punishment
jocosely	unconventional behavior
chastisement	hereditary
likely	counterpart
thing that resembles another	deeply respectful

Review: Units 7 & 8

Contrasts

"Inclined" and "prone" (Unit 4) are closely synonymous. Both refer to a tendency or likelihood to think, feel, or act a certain way. There are some differences in usage, however. "Inclined" is used to describe a momentary tendency, while "prone" conveys more of a habitual state of mind. Here are some examples:

1. "I am inclined to eat this slice of cake."

2. "I am prone to eating too much cake."

In the examples above, "inclined" and "prone" could not be substituted for each other.

Like "prone," "inclined" also has a concrete meaning, in that it can describe something that is slanted relative to another surface (e.g., a ramp can be described as an inclined plane).

Fast facts

1. The adverb "jocosely" comes from a Latin word meaning "full of jokes." The adjectival form is "jocular." Thus, a person who is behaving jocosely can be described as jocular. The adjective "jocular" is in turn similar in meaning to the word "jovial," although the words have a different origin. "Jovial" is a reference to the Roman god Jupiter (also known as Jove)—a jovial person is one who is merry, or good-humored, like Jupiter.

2. The word "chastisement" comes from a Latin word that means "to make pure," as if to suggest that punishment can "purify" someone of wrong-doing. Currently "chastisement" refers primarily to verbal punishment (e.g., scolding). The Latin root can be seen in other English words such as "chaste," which means pure, or virginal, and "chastened," which can mean tamed or restrained. A person becomes chastened by negative experiences, such as failure or punishment. Thus, one could say that when *chastisement* is successful, the person who was *chastised* will be *chastened*.

■ Grammar stretches

Instructions: Fill in the blank in each sentence below with one of the words from the following list. You may have to change the grammatical form of each word in order for it to fit into a sentence.

chastisement	counterpart	eccentricity	hereditary	inclined
jocosely	reverent	stolidity	whimsical	

1. One sees a great deal of _____ among people when they enter the Sistine Chapel for the first time.

2. The fact that my new neighbor owns at least fifteen cats and a parrot was the first sign that she is a bit _____.

3. The flight attendant remained calm during the thunderstorm and answered passengers' questions with matter-of-fact, _____ responses.

4. Boris was a _____ man who loved to laugh and tell funny stories.

5. Barbara was severely _____ for breaking her mother's favorite lamp.

6. Our personal characteristics can be attributed to the way we are raised as well as to _____.

7. His two _____ in the other law firm did not agree with his assessment of this particular case.

8. When I was a child, my father's bedtime stories were full of _____ and fantastic adventure.

9. Raul's _____ was to doubt what the customer service representative was telling him about the warranty on his stove.

Error watch

Instructions: In the following sentences, note whether the underlined word is used correctly or not. Circle the **C** at the end of the sentence if the word is used correctly; circle the **I** if it is used incorrectly.

1. Her interest in a second job was motivated by *pecuniary* concerns.   C   I

2. The *torpor* among the surgeons that morning helped them focus more carefully on the patient.   C   I

3. The vase was unusually *stolid*, and thus it did not break when it was dropped.   C   I

4. Classical music has a *soporific* effect on some people but a more stimulating effect on others.   C   I

5. Jacob's periodic fasts and solemn pre-dawn meditation rituals are part of why he is considered such a *jocose* person.   C   I

6. From her *whimsical* remarks, one could tell that she took the memorial service quite seriously.   C   I

7. I am *inclined* to say that the weather will turn cold tomorrow.   C   I

■ Matching

Instructions: Draw a line between words that have the same meaning.

unconventional behavior	monetary
inherited	stolidity
pecuniary	sleep-producing
reverent	inclined
likely	with humor
whimsical	torpor
emotionlessness	deeply respectful
punishment	eccentricity
thing that resembles another	playful
soporific	chastisement
jocosely	counterpart
listlessness	hereditary

Unit 9

New words

Cogent	Fervid
Consummate	Loquacious
Credulousness	Prevarication
Disabuse	Spurious
Dissemble	

From inference to meaning

Instructions: Read the following passage and use contextual information to guess the meanings of the underlined words. Then, have a look at the table below to see how accurately you guessed the meanings.

If you think Ingram was an honest man, let me <u>disabuse</u> you right now of that idea. Although he was quite honest in appearance, Ingram had an amazing ability to <u>dissemble</u> whenever needed. In his lifetime he had been an astronaut and a poet, a doctor and a lawyer, a social worker and a spy, shifting with ease from one occupation to the other depending on who he was addressing. In truth he had done none of those things; he was merely a <u>fervid</u> liar. Whereas most liars are vague or inconsistent on key details, Ingram's lies were clear and <u>cogent</u>, and his logic was unassailable. Somehow he always knew exactly how much to say: With one person he would be brief, slipping lies into the conversation with minimal commentary; with another he would be <u>loquacious</u>, introducing detail after detail—all of which were <u>spurious</u>. In some cases, when he was talking to uncritical and easily persuaded listeners, his success as a liar could be attributed to their <u>credulousness</u>. In most cases, it was not the listener but rather Ingram's own <u>consummate</u> skill at <u>prevarication</u> that guaranteed the success of his lies.

Your guesses

Cogent: _____   Fervid: _____

Consummate: _____   Loquacious: _____

Credulousness: _____   Prevarication: _____

Disabuse: _____   Spurious: _____

Dissemble: _____

Definitions

Cogent: well-reasoned; convincing

Consummate: masterful; complete

Credulousness: gullibility

Disabuse: correct a mistaken belief

Dissemble: deceive; create false impression

Fervid: passionate

Loquacious: talkative

Prevarication: lying

Spurious: false

■ Word fuse

Instructions: Draw a line between each fragment in the left column and one fragment in the right column to create a word.

LOQU	VID
CRED	BUSE
SPU	ACIOUS
FER	RIOUS
CO	CATION
DIS	ULOUSNESS
CONSU	GENT
PREVARI	SEMBLE
DISA	MMATE

▪ Fill-ins

Instructions: Fill in the blank in each sentence below with one of the words from the following list:

> cogent   consummate   credulousness   disabuse   dissemble
> fervid   loquacious   prevarication   spurious

1. She accused my brother of _____, but in fact he had made an honest mistake.

2. Alice is a _____ chef, capable of creating not only delicious entrees but also appetizers, side dishes, and desserts.

3. Someone should gently _____ Mike of his belief that he will be a professional basketball player someday, he is too small and too slow.

4. Because the Senator had never been to Florida, the claim that he had been arrested once in Miami was completely _____.

5. Kyle is a _____ writer; sometimes he will work on an essay for three or four hours straight without moving from his desk.

6. She persuaded me to think her way because her arguments were so _____ and clear.

7. The Jenkins family was easily swindled by the con man due to their _____.

8. Tell me what happened; you don't need to _____ anymore.

9. Although he was an eloquent speaker, Jones also tended to be _____, and so his speeches often ran longer than scheduled.

■ Word scramble

Instructions: Unscramble each of the following words. Use the hints below as needed.

1) E S I U A D B S _____

2) R S U I U S O P _____

3) U U O O A L C S I Q _____

4) T G E O N C _____

5) P A V I T N A R C R I E O _____

6) I F D V R E _____

7) S I L M E D E S B _____

8) D C S O E R S U E U N S L _____

9) S M O N C E A U T M _____

Hints:
1) correct a mistaken belief, 2) false, 3) talkative, 4) well-reasoned, 5) lying, 6) passionate,
7) deceive, 8) gullibility, 9) masterful

■ Matching

Instructions: Draw a line between words that have the same meaning.

false	loquacious
talkative	dissemble
consummate	correct a mistaken belief
fervid	lying
well-reasoned	credulousness
prevarication	spurious
disabuse	passionate
gullibility	masterful
deceive	cogent

Unit 10

New words

Assiduously	Unassailable
Inept	Undaunted
Onerous	

From inference to meaning

Instructions: Read the following passage and use contextual information to guess the meanings of the underlined words. Then, have a look at the table below to see how accurately you guessed the meanings.

Night after night, the physics teacher stayed up late, working assiduously on lesson plans for her class. She knew that mastering the material was an onerous task for many of the students, as most of them lacked a solid foundation in math and science. However, she was undaunted by their lack of knowledge and skills. She had faith in her own ability to help even the most inept students overcome their limitations, and so each night she devoted herself to her lesson plans. Her confidence that she could teach the students physics was unassailable.

Your guesses

Assiduously: _____   Unassailable: _____

Inept: _____   Undaunted: _____

Onerous: _____

Definitions

Assiduously: diligently; persistently

Inept: incompetent; awkward

Onerous: burdensome

Unassailable: impossible to attack; unalterable

Undaunted: not discouraged; resolute

■ Word fuse

Instructions: Draw a line between each fragment in the left column and one fragment in the right column to create a word.

IN	EROUS
AS	DAUNTED
UNA	EPT
ON	SIDUOUSLY
UN	SSAILABLE

■ Fill-ins

Instructions: Fill in the blank in each sentence below with one of the words from the following list:

assiduously   inept   onerous   unassailable   undaunted

1. She continued to drive toward Anchorage, _____ by the blizzard that was raging outside the car.

2. Trey guessed that the plumber was _____, because when he got home he saw that his basement was knee-deep in water.

3. Reading this chapter in my calculus book is such an _____ task!

4. The attorney's closing statement swayed the jury in her client's favor; she spoke with passion, and her logic was _____.

5. Richard studied _____ that night so that he wouldn't fail his history test the next morning.

■ Word scramble

Instructions: Unscramble each of the following words. Use the hints below as needed.

1) U S I B A N L A S E A L _____

2) R E U O S N O _____

3) S U I A O U S D Y L S _____

4) P I E N T _____

5) U E T D U N N A D _____

Hints:
1) impossible to attack, 2) burdensome, 3) diligently, 4) incompetent, 5) not discouraged

■ Matching

Instructions: Draw a line between words that have the same meaning.

inept   impossible to attack

burdensome   undaunted

not discouraged   incompetent

unassailable   assiduously

diligently   onerous

Review: Units 9 & 10

Contrasts

1. The adjectives "loquacious" and "garrulous" (unit 5) are synonyms.

2. The adjectives "undaunted" and "resolute" (unit 4) are similar in meaning, as both refer to a person who is unshakeable when challenged. In some cases they are interchangeable. However, the two words also differ in usage. "Undaunted" is more commonly used when the challenge is relatively extreme and immediately present. "Resolute" is more commonly used to refer to a person's beliefs. For example:

   The soldier continued to hold her ground, *undaunted* by the bullets whistling around her ears. She was *resolute* in her faith that the bullets would not hit her.

3. The verbs "prevaricate" and "dissemble" are similar in meaning, in that both refer to deliberate attempts to deceive. However, the meanings of the two words also differ slightly. To prevaricate is to tell a lie. In other words, it is an attempt to deceive by verbal means. To dissemble is to be deceptive using any means, verbal or nonverbal, specifically for the purpose of creating a false impression. For example:

   In order to stay home from school, the child had been *dissembling* a serious illness all morning. He kept clutching his stomach, moaning, and *prevaricating* about various non-existent aches and pains.

Fast facts

1. The word "consummate" comes from a Latin word that means "complete." As an adjective, consummate refers to someone that is "complete" in the sense of having mastered all elements in a domain (e.g., a consummate chef is one who is capable of excellence in all sorts of cooking). As a verb, "consummate" refers specifically to the

"completion" of a marriage through sexual intercourse. A marriage is said to be consummated when the couple has intercourse.

2. The word "assiduous" comes from the Latin words "ad" (to) and "sedere" (sit). Assiduous people can be thought of as sitting down to concentrate diligently on their work. However, a person does not need to be seated to be assiduous. A police officer, for instance, might be described as assiduously directing the flow of traffic during a crowded and somewhat chaotic public event. The Latin verb "sedere" appears in other English words too. For example, the word "sedulous" is a synonym for "assiduous." "Sediment" is the solid matter that "sits" at the bottom of a liquid. And, a "sedentary" person is a person who engages in very little physical activity, perhaps because he or she spends a great deal of time in a seated position. For example:

Paula's mother always told her: "It's good to be *sedulous* with your work, but don't be *sedentary*."

Grammar stretches

Instructions: Fill in the blank in each sentence below with one of the words from the following list. You may have to change the grammatical form of each word in order for it to fit into a sentence.

> assiduously   cogent   credulousness   disabuse   fervid   inept
> loquacious   onerous   prevarication   spurious   undaunted

1. Imani almost succeeded in _____ Matthew of the notion that school is a waste of time.

2. Luke played guitar _____, often breaking strings due to the intensity of his playing.

3. The more you _____, the less people are inclined to trust you.

4. In spite of intense heat, snakes, and thick mud, the explorers continued to proceed _____ through the jungle.

5. The day he lost a quarter of a million dollars in bad investments, George's colleagues realized the full extent of his _____ in business matters.

6. If you are _____ in your work, you will surely succeed.

7. A good argument has the quality of _____; it will seem as if it could never be proven false.

8. In his article, the author was guilty of considerable _____, as he made six claims that were later proven to be untrue.

9. Brittany is much too _____; I think she should be a more skeptical person rather than believing everything she hears.

10. Paul is thinking of quitting his job due to the _____ of his responsibilities.

11. In the midst of another long, overly wordy lecture, Darren began to grow weary of the instructor's _____.

■ Error watch

Instructions: In the following sentences, note whether the underlined word is used correctly or not. Circle the **C** at the end of the sentence if the word is used correctly; circle the **I** if it is used incorrectly.

1. Mark is a <u>consummate</u> mechanic, as he doesn't know the first thing about cars.   C   I

2. The logic underlying your term paper is clear and <u>undaunted</u>.   C   I

3. After being treated badly by her foster parents, the child was relocated to another home where the process of <u>disabuse</u> could take place.   C   I

4. Evidence that the student had plagiarized Smith's book was <u>unassailable</u>; thus, he was expelled.   C   I

5. Jim began to fill out his federal income tax form, a lengthy activity that he found to be quite <u>onerous</u>.   C   I

6. The politician's speech was filled with half-truths and outright <u>prevarications</u>.   C   I

7. Thanks to her <u>credulousness</u>, Diane was able to finish the homework assignment much more quickly than her parents had expected.   C   I

▮ Matching

Instructions: Draw a line between words that have the same meaning.

onerous	masterful
dissemble	well-reasoned
passionate	lying
inept	loquacious
consummate	incompetent
unassailable	deceive
disabuse	fervid
cogent	gullibility
diligently	not discouraged
prevarication	spurious
credulousness	impossible to attack
false	assiduously
talkative	burdensome
undaunted	correct a mistaken belief

Unit 11

Craven   Obsequious

Encomium   Quisling

Exonerate   Transgressions

Magnanimous   Vilified

Nefarious

From inference to meaning

Instructions: Imagine for a moment that a political figure has made contro-
versial statements about immigration reform resulting in some people calling him an unpatriotic man and even a traitor. One of his colleagues decides
to make a speech in his defense. The colleague consults with a speechwriter
who gives her recommendations about what to say and how to say it. Read
the speechwriter's recommendations below and guess the meanings of the
underlined words. (You will see that in each sentence, the underlined word
contrasts in meaning with another key word in the sentence.) Then, have a
look at the table below to see how accurately you guessed the meanings.

> As you know, the goal of your speech is to <u>exonerate</u> the man
> rather than to blame him. Start by acknowledging that for the most part he
> has been <u>vilified</u> rather than praised for his recent statements. Then build
> your case. Remind your audience that for many years he had the reputa-
> tion of being a patriot, not a <u>quisling</u>. Share some anecdotes illustrating
> how he was benevolent rather than <u>nefarious</u>, <u>magnanimous</u> rather than
> petty, and courageous rather than <u>craven</u>. In sum, present an <u>encomium</u>
> rather than merely a defense. But don't be <u>obsequious</u>; your audience will
> be more responsive if you're blunt with them about his most admirable
> qualities as well as his <u>transgressions</u>.

Your guesses

Craven: _____   Obsequious: _____

Encomium: _____   Quisling: _____

Exonerate: _____   Transgressions: _____

Magnanimous: _____   Vilified: _____

Nefarious: _____

Definitions

Craven: cowardly

Encomium: a tribute; a formal expression of praise

Exonerate: free from blame; absolve

Magnanimous: generous and noble

Nefarious: wicked

Obsequious: overly eager to please; servile

Quisling: traitor; collaborator

Transgressions: misdeeds; crimes

Vilified: maligned; spoken very badly of

Word fuse

Instructions: Draw a line between each fragment in the left column and one fragment in the right column to create a word.

EXO	FIED
QUIS	MIUM
OBSE	NERATE
CRA	ARIOUS
NEF	LING
TRANS	QUIOUS
ENCO	GRESSIONS
VILI	ANIMOUS
MAGN	VEN

Fill-ins

Instructions: Fill in the blank in each sentence below with one of the words from the following list:

craven	encomium	exonerate	magnanimous
nefarious	obsequious	quisling	transgressions
vilified			

1. According to historical accounts, the king was a _____ man who betrayed both friends and enemies without remorse.

2. The tribal court found the young woman guilty of numerous _____.

3. Jill had a disturbingly _____ way of trying to win favor with authority figures.

4. I'll never know the identity of the _____ person who left an insulting note on my desk but wasn't brave enough to sign it.

5. The dictator was _____ by the press for many decades of oppressive policies.

6. After her father passed away, Reika prepared an _____ to be read at the memorial service in order to honor his memory.

7. Benedict Arnold was a well-known _____ who had been an American general before defecting to the British Army.

8. How _____ of her to forgive her ex-husband for years of neglect and hurtful behavior!

9. Although he appears to be guilty, a closer look at the evidence will surely _____ the defendant.

■ Word scramble

Instructions: Unscramble each of the following words. Use the hints below as needed.

1) I S Q S U U E B O O _____

2) U A G M N O A S N I M _____

3) I D I I E V F L _____

4) L S I U N G I Q _____

5) V R N C E A _____

6) S N A R O E U I F _____

7) T E X E R E N O A _____

8) S R O A N S S S G R N E I T _____

9) C E M N M U I O _____

Hints:
1) overly eager to please, 2) generous and noble, 3) maligned, 4) traitor, 5) cowardly,
6) wicked, 7) free from blame, 8) misdeeds, 9) tribute

Matching

Instructions: Draw a line between words that have the same meaning.

vilified	misdeeds
encomium	cowardly
transgressions	free from blame
obsequious	maligned
quisling	wicked
craven	generous and noble
exonerate	traitor
magnanimous	overly eager to please
nefarious	tribute

Unit 12

New words

Aristocratic

Canon

Prolific

Tome

Unabated

Venerated

From inference to meaning

Instructions: Read the following passage and use contextual information to guess the meanings of the underlined words. Then, have a look at the table below to see how accurately you guessed the meanings.

Leo Tolstoy was an exceptionally underlined prolific author, having written dozens of novels, stories, plays, and essays during a long life that spanned most of the nineteenth century. His most celebrated work of fiction, *War and Peace*, is a massive tome, written in both Russian and French, that focuses on the lives of five aristocratic families during the period of time leading up to the French invasion of Russia. First published in 1869, the book was an almost instant classic, and its popularity has continued almost unabated to the present day. No doubt there will always be a place in the canon of Western literature for this powerful, venerated work.

Your guesses

Aristocratic: _____   Tome: _____

Canon: _____   Unabated: _____

Prolific: _____   Venerated: _____

Definitions

Aristocratic: noble

Canon: representative works

Prolific: highly productive; fecund

Tome: scholarly book

Unabated: continued at full strength

Venerated: deeply respected; revered

Word fuse

Instructions: Draw a line between each fragment in the left column and one fragment in the right column to create a word.

CAN	BATED
UNA	OCRATIC
TO	ON
PROL	RATED
ARIST	IFIC
VENE	ME

Fill-ins

Instructions: Fill in the blank in each sentence below with one of the words from the following list:

aristocratic   canon   prolific   tome   unabated   venerated

1. _____ even after three hours, the storm continued to batter the little house.

2. My dog walks around with such a regal expression, you would think she had an _____ background.

3. Scholars have yet to agree about the authorship of some of the works in the Shakespearean _____.

4. The old general was _____ by his troops.

5. She was a _____ artist, often producing as many as three canvases per week.

6. Last year, Jackson published a massive _____ summarizing the major battles of the U.S. Civil War.

Word scramble

Instructions: Unscramble each of the following words. Use the hints below as needed.

1) O I C L I R F P _____

2) S C I A O T T R R C A I _____

3) T E E N A E D R V _____

4) D N A T U A B E _____

5) A C N N O _____

6) M O T E _____

Hints:
1) highly productive, 2) noble, 3) deeply respected, 4) continued at full strength,
5) representative works, 6) scholarly book

■ Matching

Instructions: Draw a line between words that have the same meaning.

noble   scholarly book

representative works   venerated

tome   continued at full strength

prolific   canon

unabated   aristocratic

deeply respected   highly productive

Review: Units 11 & 12

Contrasts

The word "vilify" is similar in meaning to "berate" and "impugn" (both of which are introduced in Unit 3) in that each of these words implies a verbal attack. At the same time, there are some differences between their meanings:

1. To berate is to verbally attack a person. For example, "She berated me for having forgotten her birthday." As this example illustrates, the attack is communicated to the person. The purpose is to express frustration or anger to the person.

2. To impugn is to verbally attack a person's ideas or reputation. The purpose is to show that the ideas are inaccurate or inappropriate, or that the reputation is undeserved. For example, "He impugned her reputation as a teacher."

3. To vilify is to verbally attack a person in order to hurt them or undermine their reputation. For example, "She was vilified by Smith in his most recent article." As this example illustrates, the attack is not communicated directly to the person.

Fast facts

1. The adjective "magnanimous" is a combination of the Latin words "magnus" (great) and "animus" (soul). Thus, to describe someone as magnanimous is to call them, literally, "great-souled." The Latin root "magnus" appears in many English words. For example, the honorific phrase "magna cum laude" means "with great praise." (The order of the words in Latin is, literally, "great with praise.") Other words that begin with "mag" and have something to do with greatness or great size include *magnificent* and *magnum*. A "magnate" is a person of great power and influence. For example:

   As he was a *magnate* in the steel industry, he could afford to have a *magnificent* house built for himself and his family.

2. The noun "canon" comes from a Greek word meaning "standard." In the passage about Tolstoy, "canon" refers to a representative group of written works. Thus, one could refer to the canon of Western literature, the canon of 18th-century French essays, or the canon of one particular writer. "Canon" could also refer specifically to those works from one genre or author that are considered genuine—for example, one could refer to the Shakespearean canon, meaning just those works that are agreed to have been written by Shakespeare rather than by someone else. "Canon" also has other meanings as well. For example, it can be used to refer to a generally accepted principle (as in the canons of domestic law), a type of song, or a type of prayer.

◼ Grammar stretches

Instructions: Fill in the blank in each sentence below with one of the words from the following list. You may have to change the grammatical form of each word in order for it to fit into a sentence.

aristocratic	craven	exonerate	magnanimous	nefarious
obsequious	prolific	quisling	tome	venerated
vilified				

1. The regime demonstrated a capacity for murder, theft, and other forms of _____.

2. Professor Carter finally managed to publish the two massive _____ she had been working on for six years.

3. A nation cannot survive if it contains too many _____ betraying its interests.

4. Not many people composed music as _____ as he did; by mid-career he had already written more than two hundred songs.

5. During election years, the popular media always _____
at least one candidate for bad behavior or unappealing views, thereby
undermining the candidate's appeal.

6. Donald always tried to flatter people in positions of power; for years
his wife had put up with his _____.

7. I think that George acted _____ when he abandoned his
comrades in the middle of the battle.

8. After a lengthy discussion with her boss, Maria was finally
_____ of the mistake she had supposedly made, and
her boss apologized for initially believing that Maria had been in
the wrong.

9. Although her brother often let her down, Selma always responded with
great _____, forgiving him for his faults while treating him
with kindness and generosity.

10. Even if you did not know they were princes, you would recognize that
the two brothers were _____ by the noble way they carried
themselves.

11. After a long career of public service and good works, he is deserving
of our _____.

■ Error watch

Instructions: In the following sentences, note whether the underlined word is used correctly or not. Circle the C at the end of the sentence if the word is used correctly; circle the I if it is used incorrectly.

1. Mrs. Lyman has held season tickets to the opera for three decades and has never missed a performance; even after all these years, her passion for operatic performances continues <u>unabated</u>.   C   I

2. Wilson's first book was a lengthy <u>canon</u> on the topic of modern British history.   C   I

3. It was most <u>nefarious</u> of the man to forgive his enemies and treat them as equals in spite of their hostility.   C   I

4. Last year Lan wrote an <u>encomium</u> that spoke of her grandfather in the most glowing, reverential terms.   C   I

5. He was the most <u>venerated</u> political figure of his generation, widely disliked for his policies as well as for his personal shortcomings.   C   I

6. The man's <u>obsequiousness</u> was evident in the way he trembled every time he heard a loud noise.   C   I

7. Everyone <u>exonerated</u> him for his crimes, because nobody considered the possibility that he was innocent.   C   I

8. Matthews can no longer be considered a <u>prolific</u> writer, given that he has only written one screenplay and a couple of essays during the past ten years.   C   I

■ Matching

Instructions: Draw a line between words that have the same meaning.

highly productive	representative works
magnanimous	vilified
continued at full strength	misdeeds
canon	venerated
noble	scholarly book
traitor	nefarious
overly eager to please	aristocratic
deeply respected	prolific
maligned	encomium
tribute	craven
transgressions	obsequious
wicked	free from blame
tome	unabated
cowardly	generous and noble
exonerate	quisling

■ Word Search

Instructions: All of the new words from Units 11 and 12 are hidden in this challenging puzzle. The words may be written forwards or backwards in any direction: horizontal, vertical, or diagonal. Some words overlap in one letter. Your task is to circle each word once you have found it.

Following are the meanings of the words you're looking for. (Remember: You're searching for the actual words, not the meanings given here.)

overly eager to please	generous and noble	maligned
traitor	cowardly	wicked
free from blame	misdeeds	tribute
highly productive	noble	deeply respected
representative works	scholarly book	continued at full strength

```
R I W N M O O F E A Q U I S L I N G A U
E X O N E R A T E S F H L R A D E E N N
T I C I F I L O R P L E A P O U R A L M
S O O L W E R M P B Q U R T S E B L I H
O D E E L L T E O U P U O E A O O M F
S B A E W T E R R O C R F N T U R U K E
E Y T D I L N C Y L L E E X Q I R O E
N O Y A A O O R O N O C D F T A T A E S
M I B R N M A Y I E A N L A C E I L L A
I G I S N V E R L D E T A R E N E V L D
A N M T E N E I E E I O I I V O X I S H
R Y A N L Q A A L I M O M O T R E S A O
N M E A Z R U R A N E E Y U V L S B L E
M A L L I E T I S D G E I S I D I N A N
I G T G M I K S O E N T I N G E B R Y C
C N H Q U A L T E U I Y U O H I A R E O
U A W G J N E O I L S P E A L F L G T M
S N N O Z S I C E R C E X T I I E E N I
F I E O L O X R V E M L E M S L R N D U
I M L R N E I A E H I A E N N I T N S M
E O B E B S E T Z O X G R N I V U U E E
W U E T A O S I W K L I L E F R O L R E
A S I G O A A C O N H Y T R A E D L G A
M L E E R N S N O I S S E R G S N A R T
```

ANSWER KEY: CHAPTER 1

Unit 1

Word fuse

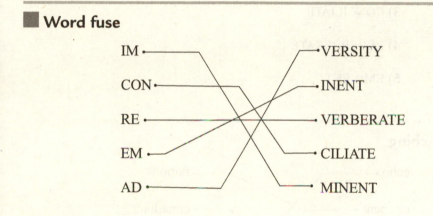

IM ———→ INENT

CON ———→ VERSITY

RE ———→ VERBERATE

EM ———→ MINENT

AD ———→ CILIATE

Fill-ins

1. Once the thunder and lightning started, we knew that rain was _**imminent**_.

2. It is easier to aggravate a person than it is to _**conciliate**_ him or her.

3. His was a life filled with _**adversity**_, having spent time in jail on three separate occasions, and then finding it difficult to convince employers to hire him.

4. Sheronica could hear the sound of the engine _**reverberate**_ in the cool autumn air.

5. Who do you consider the most _**eminent**_ researcher in the field of genetic engineering?

◼ Word scramble

1) ADVERSITY

2) IMMINENT

3) CONCILIATE

4) REVERBERATE

5) EMINENT

◼ Matching

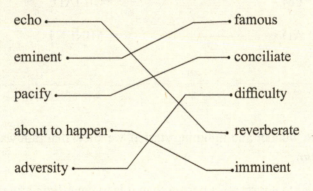

Unit 2

Word fuse

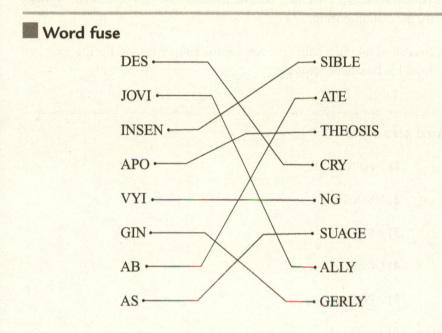

DES	SIBLE
JOVI	ATE
INSEN	THEOSIS
APO	CRY
VYI	NG
GIN	SUAGE
AB	ALLY
AS	GERLY

Fill-ins

1. With a big smile and a warm hug, my uncle greeted me **_jovially_**.

2. Linda wasn't able to **_assuage_** her father's concerns about her recent car trouble.

3. Although the grass beside the lake was tall and dense, the hunter believed that while hiding there he would still be able to **_descry_** the ducks as they landed on the water.

4. With her straight-A average and her prowess on the soccer field, Mary is the **_apotheosis_** of the scholar-athlete.

5. The effects of the illness rendered the young man almost completely **_insensible_**.

6. After injuring my foot, I had to walk very ***gingerly***.

7. Two hours into the spelling bee, there were still four contestants ***vying*** for the championship.

8. Instead of taking a pain reliever, Carlos simply waited for the pain from his headache to ***abate***.

■ Word scramble

1) INSENSIBLE

2) VYING

3) ABATE

4) GINGERLY

5) APOTHEOSIS

6) JOVIALLY

7) DESCRY

8) ASSUAGE

■ Matching

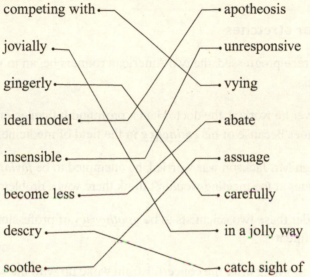

competing with ——————— apotheosis

jovially ——————— unresponsive

gingerly ——————— vying

ideal model ——————— abate

insensible ——————— assuage

become less ——————— carefully

descry ——————— in a jolly way

soothe ——————— catch sight of

Review: Units 1 & 2

■ Grammar stretches

1. As the race progressed, the two American runners began to ***vie*** for the lead.

2. Wherever he worked, the doctor had a profound influence on his colleagues because of his ***eminence*** in the field of medicine.

3. Although Mr. Jackson was worried, he attempted to be ***jovial*** so that his colleagues at the meeting wouldn't think there was a problem.

4. I consider these two scientists to be ***apotheoses*** of professional commitment.

5. On the morning after the concert, Efrain woke up with the sounds of electric guitars still ***reverberating*** in his head.

6. She has the capacity to succeed no matter how ***adverse*** her circumstances.

7. What concerns me most about the economic downturn she predicted for next month is not its magnitude but rather its ***imminence***.

8. Long after the flooding had ***abated***, the citizens continued to deal with the aftermath of the storm.

9. Rather than adopting a ***conciliatory*** attitude, Rosemary met her critic's hostility with some angry words of her own.

10. I spoke as reassuringly as I could, but I'm not sure whether I ***assuaged*** her fears.

11. The soldiers watched the sky carefully until they had ***descried*** a plane.

12. As the man became more intoxicated and unable to comprehend what we were telling him, he began to speak more and more ***insensibly***.

■ Error watch

1. Even if she holds her son's hand during a visit to the dentist, she is unable to <u>descry</u> his fear.   **Incorrect**

2. When the plumber banged on the pipes, a clanging sound <u>reverberated</u> all around the building.   **Correct**

3. People all over the world recognized this <u>imminent</u> actor whenever he made an appearance.   **Incorrect**

4. Due to his inexperience, the employee didn't know how to <u>abate</u> the angry customer.   **Incorrect**

5. Emilio grew up in a loving, happy, and rather sheltered environment; as a result, he considered himself fairly inexperienced at dealing with <u>adversity</u>.   **Correct**

6. Abraham Lincoln is one of America's most <u>apotheosis</u> political figures.   **Incorrect**

Matching

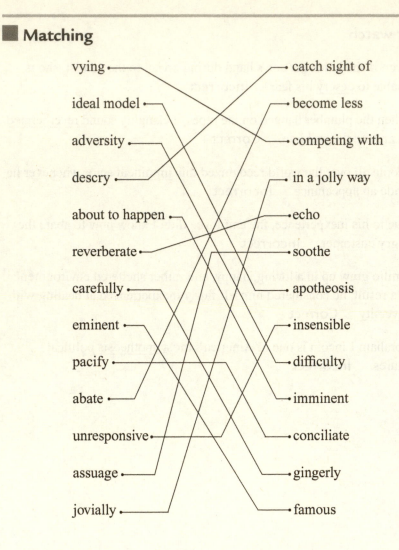

vying

ideal model

adversity

descry

about to happen

reverberate

carefully

eminent

pacify

abate

unresponsive

assuage

jovially

catch sight of

become less

competing with

in a jolly way

echo

soothe

apotheosis

insensible

difficulty

imminent

conciliate

gingerly

famous

Unit 3

Word fuse

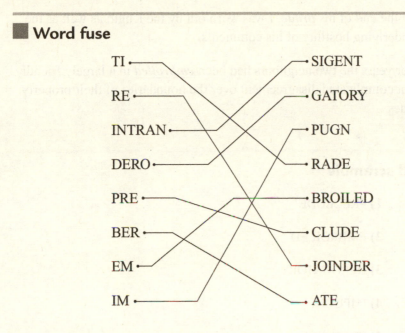

TI   SIGENT

RE   GATORY

INTRAN   PUGN

DERO   RADE

PRE   BROILED

BER   CLUDE

EM   JOINDER

IM   ATE

Fill-ins

1. We argued for two hours but neither one of us could convince the other one of anything; I guess we were both pretty ***intransigent***.

2. As Flannery O'Connor once said, "Accepting oneself does not ***preclude*** an attempt to become better."

3. He was hurt by her remarks because they were not just critical but also ***derogatory***.

4. The speaker's comments were clearly intended to ***impugn*** the reputation of the congresswoman.

5. Marta made a witty comment about John's awful haircut, but John was unable to come up with a good ***rejoinder***.

6. If you have a complaint, feel free to speak to me, but please do not **_berate_** me.

7. At the end of his **_tirade_**, I was worn out by the length as well as the underlying hostility of his comments.

8. For years the two neighbors had been **_embroiled_** in a largely friendly but complicated disagreement over the boundaries of their property lines.

■ Word scramble

1) PRECLUDE

2) EMBROILED

3) DEROGATORY

4) IMPUGN

5) REJOINDER

6) TIRADE

7) BERATE

8) INTRANSIGENT

◼ Matching

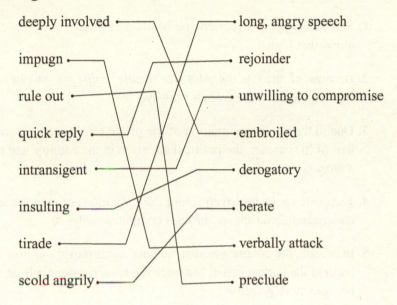

deeply involved   long, angry speech

impugn   rejoinder

rule out   unwilling to compromise

quick reply   embroiled

intransigent   derogatory

insulting   berate

tirade   verbally attack

scold angrily   preclude

◼ Unit 4

◼ Word fuse

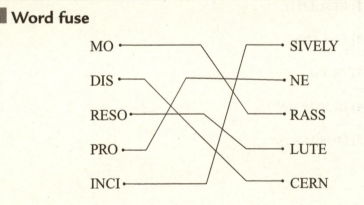

MO   SIVELY

DIS   NE

RESO   RASS

PRO   LUTE

INCI   CERN

Fill-ins

1. She was *prone* to experiencing headaches whenever her level of stress was high.

2. Because of the fog, the pilot was unable to *discern* whether the lights up ahead were from a runway.

3. Due to the abrupt resignation of the prime minister and more than half of his cabinet, the political situation in the country had become a *morass*.

4. The critic spoke *incisively* about the limitations of recent attempts to understand Shakespeare through computer analysis.

5. In private, the congresswoman seemed uncertain about how to address the budget crisis, but once the cameras were rolling she became more *resolute*.

Word scramble

1) RESOLUTE

2) DISCERN

3) PRONE

4) INCISIVELY

5) MORASS

■ Matching

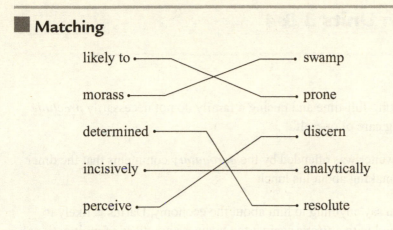

likely to ———————— swamp

morass ———————— prone

determined ———————— discern

incisively ———————— analytically

perceive ———————— resolute

Review: Units 3 & 4

■ Fill-ins

1. Working full-time and raising a family do not necessarily **_preclude_** taking care of oneself.

2. The waiter was offended by the **_derogatory_** comments that the diner kept making about his lunch.

3. If you say anything to him about the economy, Darius is likely to respond with a **_tirade_** against the business practices of multinational corporations.

4. What a **_morass_** this problem has become!

5. This particular district is **_prone_** to relatively dramatic shifts in voting preferences from election to election.

6. In spite of numerous obstacles, the teacher was **_resolute_** in her belief that this would be a good year for her students.

■ Grammar stretches

1. If you keep on **_impugning_** his reputation, he is likely to become offended.

2. No matter how often the comedian was heckled by an audience member, she always had witty **_rejoinders_**.

3. The debater was brilliant and **_incisive_** about the need for grass-roots educational reform.

4. Because he lacked the capacity for **_discernment_**, he often chose the wrong people to associate with.

5. The two archeologists were slowly *embroiling* me in their complicated dispute about who had been first to identify the lost settlement.

6. Mr. White showed so much hostility and *intransigence* in his refusal to consider our counter-offer.

7. It bothered Jasmine that the young mother had *berated* her young son for spilling the milk.

■ Error watch

1. No matter what I said, he refused to change his mind. He was so <u>discerning</u>!   Incorrect

2. Being healthy does not <u>preclude</u> the possibility of developing diabetes when one gets older.   Correct

3. I felt very <u>impugned</u> in this situation, because it demanded so much of my time and energy.   Incorrect

4. She is very <u>resolute</u> about her plan to apply to graduate school.   Correct

5. <u>Intransigence</u> will not help you get what you want from him; you need to be more cooperative.   Correct

■ Matching

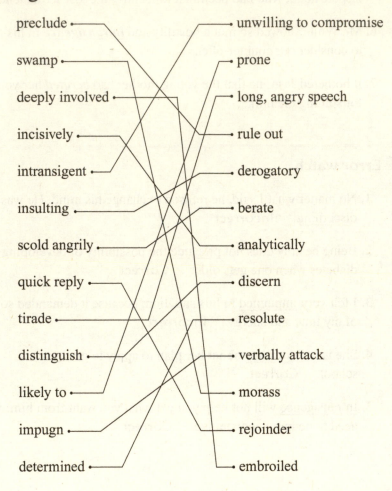

preclude   unwilling to compromise

swamp   prone

deeply involved   long, angry speech

incisively   rule out

intransigent   derogatory

insulting   berate

scold angrily   analytically

quick reply   discern

tirade   resolute

distinguish   verbally attack

likely to   morass

impugn   rejoinder

determined   embroiled

Unit 5

Word fuse

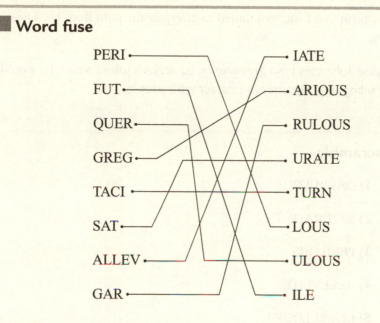

PERI————————————→ IATE

FUT————————————→ ARIOUS

QUER———————————→ RULOUS

GREG———————————→ URATE

TACI————————————→ TURN

SAT————————————→ LOUS

ALLEV——————————→ ULOUS

GAR————————————→ ILE

Fill-ins

1. Due to his **_querulous_** nature, Juan found fault will all of the solutions I proposed for his computer problem.

2. Attempting to walk across a busy freeway at night is **_perilous_**, no matter how carefully one proceeds.

3. As he scrubbed the wall, Kevin realized that any attempts to prevent tiny chips of paint from flaking off would be **_futile_**.

4. The eyewitness did not provide many details about the crime, in part because she was so **_taciturn_**.

5. Although ordinarily a man of few words, Quinton became quite **_garrulous_** once he began discussing a topic that interested him.

6. The moment she walked into the room, her perfume began to *__saturate__* the air.

7. The aspirin that Ling took failed to *__alleviate__* the pain from her knee injury.

8. Because Johannes is so *__gregarious__*, he seeks a job in which he would have many opportunities to interact with people.

Word scramble

1) GARRULOUS

2) SATURATE

3) PERILOUS

4) ALLEVIATE

5) QUERULOUS

6) GREGARIOUS

7) TACITURN

8) FUTILE

■ Matching

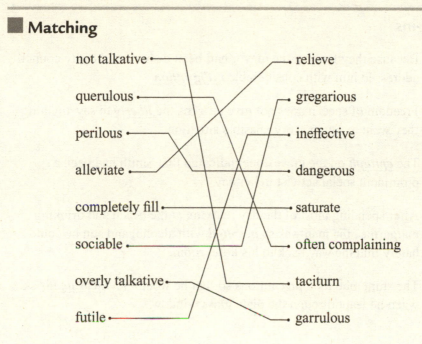

not talkative
querulous
perilous
alleviate
completely fill
sociable
overly talkative
futile

relieve
gregarious
ineffective
dangerous
saturate
often complaining
taciturn
garrulous

■ Unit 6

■ Word fuse

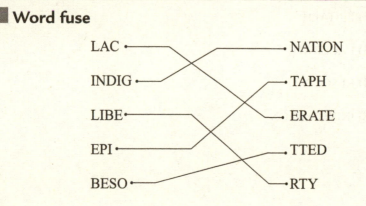

LAC
INDIG
LIBE
EPI
BESO

NATION
TAPH
ERATE
TTED
RTY

◼ Fill-ins

1. Because they felt that the mayor had been dishonest, the city council addressed him with considerable ***indignation***.

2. Freedom of speech does not give citizens the ***liberty*** to say anything they want to say in every possible situation.

3. The ***epitaph*** on the gravestone indicated that Smith had been a prominent social activist in her day.

4. After spending most of the day relaxing at the beach and drinking margaritas, the man was so ***besotted*** with alcohol and sun he could barely find the way back to his hotel room.

5. The stunt man took precautions so that he would not ***lacerate*** his skin when he leapt through the plate glass window.

◼ Word scramble

1) LIBERTY

2) EPITAPH

3) LACERATE

4) BESOTTED

5) INDIGNATION

■ Matching

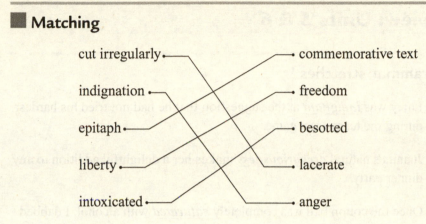

cut irregularly   commemorative text

indignation   freedom

epitaph   besotted

liberty   lacerate

intoxicated   anger

Review: Units 5 & 6

■ Grammar stretches

1. Larry was *indignant* at the suggestion that he had not tried his hardest during the team's last game.

2. Juanita's natural *gregariousness* makes her a delightful addition to any dinner party.

3. Once the cotton ball was completely *saturated* with alcohol, I dabbed the wound carefully.

4. He avoided skydiving because of the inherent *perilousness* of the activity.

5. Although the chair of the meeting asked Krystal to be brief, she addressed us most *garrulously*.

6. He finds that a hot bath goes a long way toward *alleviating* the stress of a long day's work.

7. As a result of the accident, Jace had *lacerations* on both hands and forearms.

8. One could not possibly read all of the *epitaphs* at Arlington National Cemetery.

9. There is no way John could ever be a congressman; the time he spends thinking about a congressional bid is an exercise in *futility*.

10. Talking to Jini always tried my patience due to the *querulousness* of her comments about her family and friends.

Error watch

1. After the waiter spilled a glass of water on him, Micah's shirt was almost completely <u>saturated</u>.   **Correct**

2. "You always complain when things don't go your way. I wish you were less <u>garrulous</u>!"   **Incorrect**

3. The public expressed a great deal of <u>alleviation</u> over the judge's mishandling of the case.   **Incorrect**

4. The Secret Service agent was not at <u>liberty</u> to discuss her current activities.   **Correct**

5. During their relationship, Keisha felt that Joe rarely expressed himself as much as he should have; she often wished that he would be more <u>taciturn</u>.   **Incorrect**

6. The bumblebee flew in a crooked path from flower to flower as if it were <u>besotted</u> with nectar.   **Correct**

7. Because of the civil war, it is <u>perilous</u> to visit the country at the present time.   **Correct**

8. Because he is so <u>futile</u>, it is difficult to get him to change his thinking.   **Incorrect**

■ Matching

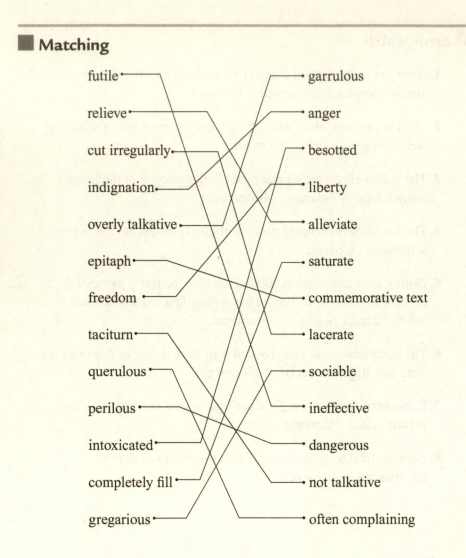

futile   garrulous

relieve   anger

cut irregularly   besotted

indignation   liberty

overly talkative   alleviate

epitaph   saturate

freedom   commemorative text

taciturn   lacerate

querulous   sociable

perilous   ineffective

intoxicated   dangerous

completely fill   not talkative

gregarious   often complaining

Word Search

```
A L I N A H P F I C T P E T E V I E O D
L T E R E O D E G R E G A R I O U S L A
L O E E M N F U N E S P T O A N D E M R
T M S U O L U R R A G E I S E G E D U S
O U I C H T T L A S W R N T R B T E L H
E Y K J A Y I O N H Q O T E A R I R I A
F T E L S O L A Y N U V I A G P O D B S
B E S O T T E D R O F U S S E U H R E T
R V L R N R E O O N I L N O K L O E R O
N E I Z E S B R X C R C A L H B A U T S
O X T L F E I S A H T U W I E O L Y Y U
E S C A S J G I Y E E N T N O D I R J O
W U E C D H I N A I R G O I G E F H O L
D O I E M O D U P P E E H E C D S E M U
A L A R S N B C O A D R A Q U A T A L R
S I L A U E T I O N S A T U R A T E I E
F R I T N E P T D I N M E T W M O M E U
G E L E T O S A Y T U R N U T O W E O Q
E P I N I E B R A L E C U L E L B R A R
R E E R O A N I N D I G N A T I O N Y I
E A R T O L K S W E E D C F A R E L N L
E M A L O K E N I Y E F O E L I T E G E
A L L E V I A T E W A R I N A E M T S U
M A L G E O U R L O I G D E N I R E U Q
```

Unit 7

Word fuse

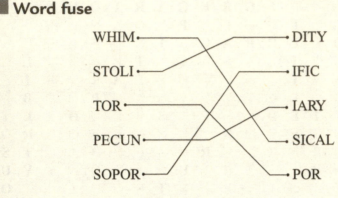

Fill-ins

1. Reading late at night has a ***soporific*** effect on some people, as it helps them fall right to sleep.

2. Karima's sudden decision to paint her room lavender was one of her more ***whimsical*** ideas.

3. When the ship grazed the iceberg, the captain's ***stolidity*** helped keep the crew from becoming overly panicked.

4. The musician was so late to his own concert that a general ***torpor*** had settled over the audience well before he took the stage.

5. As a corporate attorney, one of her responsibilities was to protect her company's ***pecuniary*** interests.

■ Word scramble

1) SOPORIFIC

2) TORPOR

3) WHIMSICAL

4) PECUNIARY

5) STOLIDITY

■ Matching

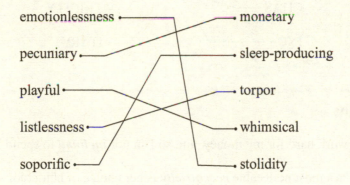

Unit 8

Word fuse

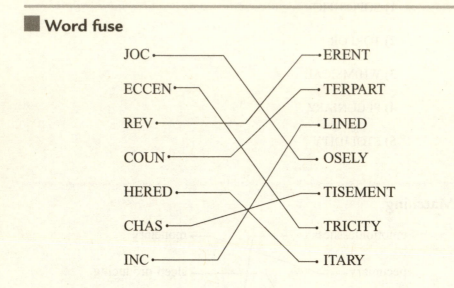

Fill-ins

1. I work hard for my money, and so I'm not *inclined* to spend it freely.

2. Nia's most noticeable *eccentricity* is her choice of hair color—orange on one side of her head, blue on the other.

3. Having studied and written about the visual arts for many years, Dwayne had a *reverent* attitude toward genuises such as Picasso.

4. I suspect that the vice president in my company makes very little money as compared to her *counterpart* in your company.

5. Melanie's hearing loss was not due to accident or illness; rather, it was *hereditary*.

6. His crimes call for more *__chastisement__* than I have the energy to deliver.

7. Though the recent firings were a serious matter, the employees in Wilma's unit treated the topic of their job security *__jocosely__*.

Word scramble

1) HEREDITARY

2) REVERENT

3) JOCOSELY

4) CHASTISEMENT

5) ECCENTRICITY

6) INCLINED

7) COUNTERPART

Matching

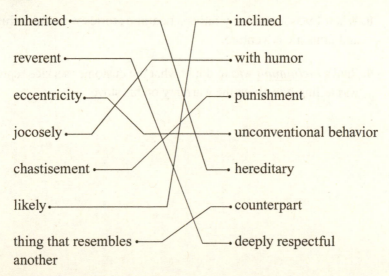

inherited
reverent
eccentricity
jocosely
chastisement
likely
thing that resembles another

inclined
with humor
punishment
unconventional behavior
hereditary
counterpart
deeply respectful

Review: Units 7 & 8

■ Grammar stretches

1. One sees a great deal of ***reverence*** among people when they enter the Sistine Chapel for the first time.

2. The fact that my new neighbor owns at least fifteen cats and a parrot was the first sign that she is a bit ***eccentric***.

3. The flight attendant remained calm during the thunderstorm and answered passengers' questions with matter-of-fact, ***stolid*** responses.

4. Boris was a ***jocose*** man who loved to laugh and tell funny stories.

5. Barbara was severely ***chastised*** for breaking her mother's favorite lamp.

6. Our personal characteristics can be attributed to the way we are raised as well as to ***heredity***.

7. His two ***counterparts*** in the other law firm did not agree with his assessment of this particular case.

8. When I was a child, my father's bedtime stories were full of ***whimsy*** and fantastic adventure.

9. Raul's ***inclination*** was to doubt what the customer service representative was telling him about the warranty on his stove.

■ Error watch

1. Her interest in a second job was motivated by <u>pecuniary</u> concerns.   Correct

2. The <u>torpor</u> among the surgeons that morning helped them focus more carefully on the patient.   Incorrect

3. The vase was unusually <u>stolid</u>, and thus it did not break when it was dropped.   Incorrect

4. Music has a <u>soporific</u> effect on some people but a more stimulating effect on others.   Correct

5. Jacob's periodic fasts and solemn pre-dawn meditation rituals are part of why he is considered such a <u>jocose</u> person.   Incorrect

6. From her <u>whimsical</u> remarks, one could tell that she took the memorial service quite seriously.   Incorrect

7. I am <u>inclined</u> to say that the weather will turn cold tomorrow.   Correct

Matching

unconventional behavior

inherited

pecuniary

reverent

likely

whimsical

emotionlessness

punishment

thing that resembles another

soporific

jocosely

listlessness

monetary

stolidity

sleep-producing

inclined

with humor

torpor

deeply respectful

eccentricity

playful

chastisement

counterpart

hereditary

Unit 9

Word fuse

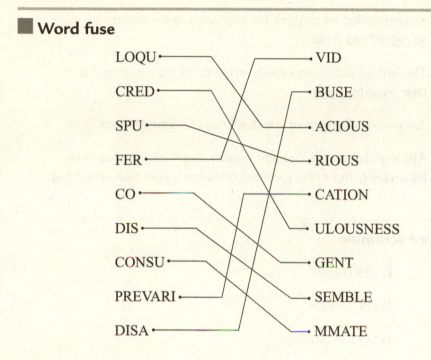

```
LOQU                    VID
CRED                    BUSE
SPU                     ACIOUS
FER                     RIOUS
CO                      CATION
DIS                     ULOUSNESS
CONSU                   GENT
PREVARI                 SEMBLE
DISA                    MMATE
```

Fill-ins

1. She accused my brother of **_prevarication_**, but in fact he had made an honest mistake.

2. Alice is a **_consummate_** chef, capable of creating not only delicious entrees but also appetizers, side dishes, and desserts.

3. Someone should gently **_disabuse_** Mike of his belief that he will be a professional basketball player someday; he is too small and too slow.

4. Because the Senator had never been to Florida, the claim that he had been arrested once in Miami was completely **_spurious_**.

5. Kyle is a *fervid* writer; sometimes he will work on an essay for three or four hours straight without moving from his desk.

6. She persuaded me to think her way because her arguments were so *cogent* and clear.

7. The Jenkins family was easily swindled by the con man due to their *credulousness*.

8. Tell me what happened; you don't need to *dissemble* anymore.

9. Although he was an eloquent speaker, Jones also tended to be *loquacious*, and so his speeches often ran longer than scheduled.

Word scramble

1) DISABUSE

2) SPURIOUS

3) LOQUACIOUS

4) COGENT

5) PREVARICATION

6) FERVID

7) DISSEMBLE

8) CREDULOUSNESS

9) CONSUMMATE

■ Matching

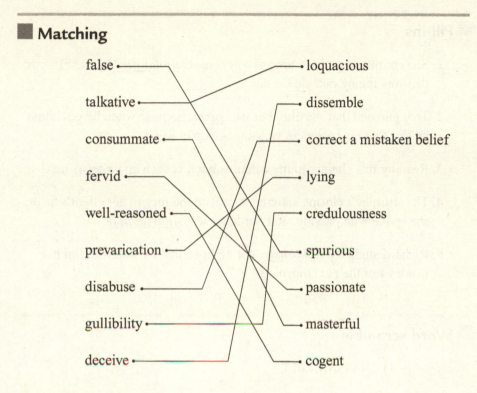

false	loquacious
talkative	dissemble
consummate	correct a mistaken belief
fervid	lying
well-reasoned	credulousness
prevarication	spurious
disabuse	passionate
gullibility	masterful
deceive	cogent

■ Unit 10

■ Word fuse

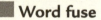

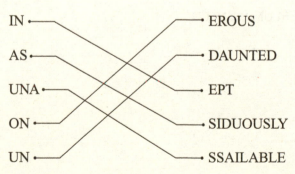

IN	EROUS
AS	DAUNTED
UNA	EPT
ON	SIDUOUSLY
UN	SSAILABLE

Fill-ins

1. She continued to drive toward Anchorage, ***undaunted*** by the blizzard that was raging outside the car.

2. Trey guessed that the plumber was ***inept***, because when he got home he saw that his basement was knee-deep in water.

3. Reading this chapter in my calculus book is such an ***onerous*** task!

4. The attorney's closing statement swayed the jury in her client's favor; she spoke with passion, and her logic was ***unassailable***.

5. Richard studied ***assiduously*** that night so that he wouldn't fail his history test the next morning.

Word scramble

1) UNASSAILABLE

2) ONEROUS

3) ASSIDUOUSLY

4) INEPT

5) UNDAUNTED

■ Matching

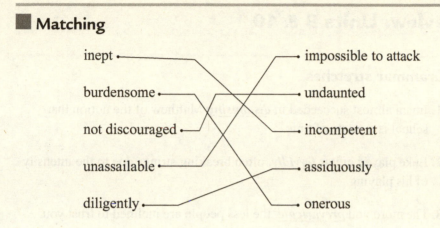

inept ——— incompetent

burdensome ——— onerous

not discouraged ——— undaunted

unassailable ——— impossible to attack

diligently ——— assiduously

Review: Units 9 & 10

■ Grammar stretches

1. Imani almost succeeded in *__disabusing__* Matthew of the notion that school is a waste of time.

2. Luke played guitar *__fervidly__*, often breaking strings due to the intensity of his playing.

3. The more you *__prevaricate__*, the less people are inclined to trust you.

4. In spite of intense heat, snakes, and thick mud, the explorers continued to proceed *__undauntedly__* through the jungle.

5. The day he lost a quarter of a million dollars in bad investments, George's colleagues realized the full extent of his *__ineptitude__* in business matters.

6. If you are *__assiduous__* in your work, you will surely succeed.

7. A good argument has the quality of *__cogency__*; it will seem as if it could never be proven false.

8. In his article, the author was guilty of considerable *__spuriousness__*, as he made six claims that were later proven to be untrue.

9. Brittany is much too *__credulous__*; I think she should be a more skeptical person rather than believing everything she hears.

10. Paul is thinking of quitting his job due to the *__onerousness__* of his responsibilities.

11. In the midst of another long, overly wordy lecture, Darren began to grow weary of the instructor's *__loquacity__*. (Or: "loquaciousness.")

■ Error watch

1. Mark is a <u>consummate</u> mechanic, as he doesn't know the first thing about cars.   **Incorrect**

2. The logic underlying your term paper is clear and <u>undaunted</u>.   **Incorrect**

3. After being treated badly by her foster parents, the child was relocated to another home where the process of <u>disabuse</u> could take place.   **Incorrect**

4. Evidence that the student had plagiarized Smith's book was <u>unassailable</u>; thus, he was expelled.   **Correct**

5. Jim began to fill out his federal income tax form, a lengthy activity that he found to be quite <u>onerous</u>.   **Correct**

6. The politician's speech was filled with half-truths and outright <u>prevarications</u>.   **Correct**

7. Thanks to her <u>credulousness</u>, Diane was able to finish the homework assignment much more quickly than her parents had expected.   **Incorrect**

■ Matching

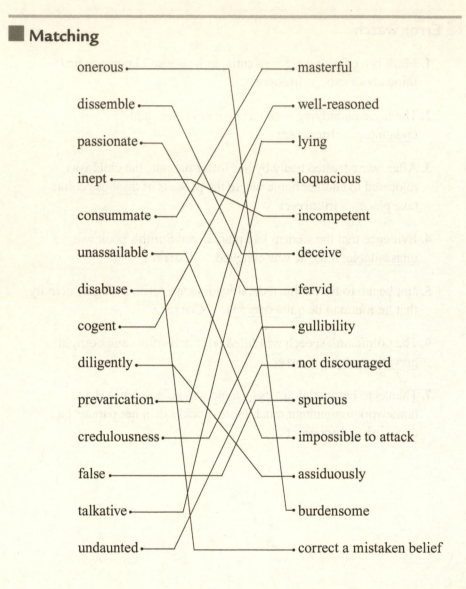

onerous   masterful

dissemble   well-reasoned

passionate   lying

inept   loquacious

consummate   incompetent

unassailable   deceive

disabuse   fervid

cogent   gullibility

diligently   not discouraged

prevarication   spurious

credulousness   impossible to attack

false   assiduously

talkative   burdensome

undaunted   correct a mistaken belief

Unit 11

Word fuse

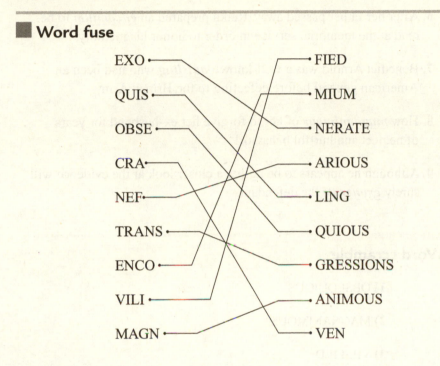

EXO   FIED

QUIS   MIUM

OBSE   NERATE

CRA   ARIOUS

NEF   LING

TRANS   QUIOUS

ENCO   GRESSIONS

VILI   ANIMOUS

MAGN   VEN

Fill-ins

1. According to historical accounts, the king was a **_nefarious_** man who betrayed both friends and enemies without remorse.

2. The tribal court found the young woman guilty of numerous **_transgressions_**.

3. Jill had a disturbingly **_obsequious_** way of trying to win favor with authority figures.

4. I'll never know the identity of the **_craven_** person who left an insulting note on my desk but wasn't brave enough to sign it.

5. The dictator was ***vilified*** by the press for many decades of oppressive policies.

6. After her father passed away, Reika prepared an ***encomium*** to be read at the memorial service in order to honor his memory.

7. Benedict Arnold was a well-known ***quisling*** who had been an American general before defecting to the British Army.

8. How ***magnanimous*** of her to forgive her ex-husband for years of neglect and hurtful behavior!

9. Although he appears to be guilty, a closer look at the evidence will surely ***exonerate*** the defendant.

Word scramble

1) OBSEQUIOUS

2) MAGNANIMOUS

3) VILIFIED

4) QUISLING

5) CRAVEN

6) NEFARIOUS

7) EXONERATE

8) TRANSGRESSIONS

9) ENCOMIUM

Matching

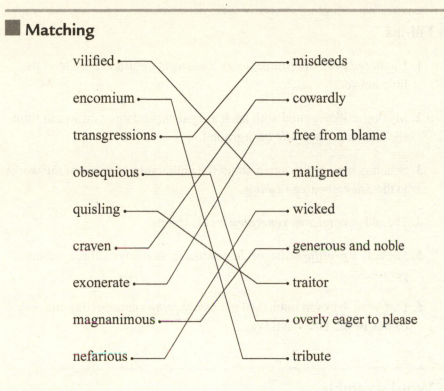

vilified
encomium
transgressions
obsequious
quisling
craven
exonerate
magnanimous
nefarious

misdeeds
cowardly
free from blame
maligned
wicked
generous and noble
traitor
overly eager to please
tribute

Unit 12

Word fuse

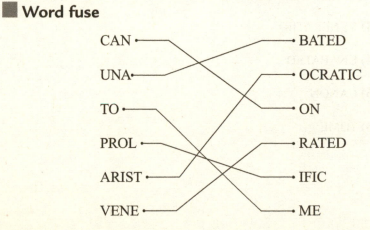

CAN
UNA
TO
PROL
ARIST
VENE

BATED
OCRATIC
ON
RATED
IFIC
ME

Fill-ins

1. *Unabated* even after three hours, the storm continued to batter the little house.

2. My dog walks around with such a regal expression, you would think she had an *aristocratic* background.

3. Scholars have yet to agree about the authorship of some of the works in the Shakespearean *canon*.

4. The old general was *venerated* by his troops.

5. She was a *prolific* artist, often producing as many as three canvases per week.

6. Last year, Jackson published a massive *tome* summarizing the major battles of the U.S. Civil War.

Word scramble

1) PROLIFIC

2) ARISTOCRATIC

3) VENERATED

4) UNABATED

5) CANON

6) TOME

■ Matching

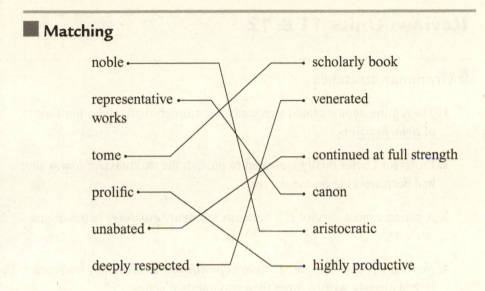

noble   scholarly book

representative works   venerated

tome   continued at full strength

prolific   canon

unabated   aristocratic

deeply respected   highly productive

Review: Units 11 & 12

■ Grammar stretches

1. The regime demonstrated a capacity for murder, theft, and other forms of ***nefariousness***.

2. Professor Carter finally managed to publish the two massive ***tomes*** she had been working on for six years.

3. A nation cannot survive if it contains too many ***quislings*** betraying its interests.

4. Not many people composed music as ***prolifically*** as he did; by mid-career he had already written more than two hundred songs.

5. During election years, the popular media always ***vilifies*** at least one candidate for bad behavior or unappealing views, thereby undermining the candidate's appeal.

6. Donald always tried to flatter people in positions of power; for years his wife had put up with his ***obsequiousness***.

7. I think that George acted ***cravenly*** when he abandoned his comrades in the middle of the battle.

8. After a lengthy discussion with her boss, Maria was finally ***exonerated*** of the mistake she had supposedly made, and her boss apologized for initially believing that Maria had been in the wrong.

9. Although her brother often let her down, Selma always responded with great ***magnanimity***, forgiving him for his faults while treating him with kindness and generosity. (Or: "magnanimousness.")

10. Even if you did not know they were princes, you would recognize that the two brothers were ***aristocrats*** by the noble way they carried themselves.

11. After a long career of public service and good works, he is deserving of our ***veneration***.

■ Error watch

1. Mrs. Lyman has held season tickets to the opera for three decades and has never missed a performance; even after all these years, her passion for operatic performances continues <u>unabated.</u>   **Correct**

2. Wilson's first book was a lengthy <u>canon</u> on the topic of modern British history.   **Incorrect**

3. It was most <u>nefarious</u> of the man to forgive his enemies and treat them as equals in spite of their hostility.   **Incorrect**

4. Last year Lan wrote an <u>encomium</u> that spoke of her grandfather in the most glowing, reverential terms.   **Correct**

5. He was the most <u>venerated</u> political figure of his generation, widely disliked for his policies as well as for his personal shortcomings.   **Incorrect**

6. The man's <u>obsequiousness</u> was evident in the way he trembled every time he heard a loud noise.   **Incorrect**

7. Everyone <u>exonerated</u> him for his crimes, because nobody considered the possibility that he was innocent.   **Incorrect**

8. Matthews can no longer be considered a <u>prolific</u> writer, given that he has only written one screenplay and a couple of essays during the past ten years.   **Correct**

◼ Matching

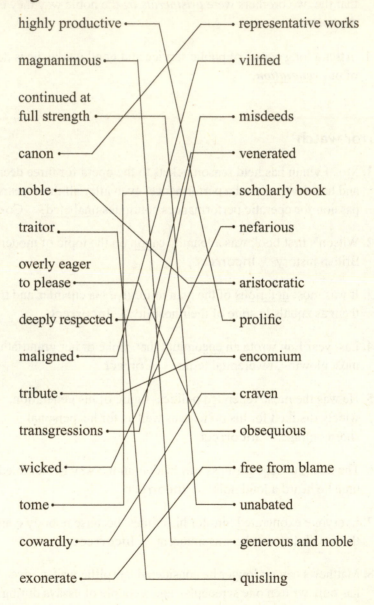

highly productive	representative works
magnanimous	vilified
continued at full strength	misdeeds
canon	venerated
noble	scholarly book
traitor	nefarious
overly eager to please	aristocratic
deeply respected	prolific
maligned	encomium
tribute	craven
transgressions	obsequious
wicked	free from blame
tome	unabated
cowardly	generous and noble
exonerate	quisling

■ Word Search

```
R I W N M O O F E A Q U I S L I N G A U
E X O N E R A T E S F H L R A D E E N N
T I C I F I L O R P L E A P O U R A L M
S O O L W E R M P B Q U R T S E B L I H
O D E E L L T E O U O P U O E A O O M F
S B A E W T E R R O C R F N T U R U K E
E Y T T D I L N C Y L L E E X Q I R O E
N O Y A A O O R O N O C D F T A T A E S
M I B R N M A Y I E A N L A C E I L L A
I G I S N V E R L D E T A R E N E V L D
A N M T E N E I E E I O I I V O X I S H
R Y A N L Q A A L I M O M O T R E S A O
N M E A Z R U R A N E E Y U V L S B L E
M A L L I E T I S D G E I S I D I N A N
I G T G M I K S O E N T I N G E B R Y C
C N H Q U A L T E U I Y U O H I A R E O
U A W G J N E O I L S P E A L F L G T M
S N N O Z S I C E R C E X T I I E E N I
F I E O L O X R V E M L E M S L R N D U
I M L R N E I A E H I A E N N I T N S M
E O B E B S E T Z O X G R N I V U U E E
W U E T A O S I W K L I L E F R O L R E
A S I G O A A C O N H Y T R A E D L G A
M L E E R N S N O I S S E R G S N A R T
```

Overview

Like Chapter 1, the purpose of this chapter is for you to learn new vocabulary. Much of this vocabulary has appeared in at least one prior version of the GRE Verbal Reasoning section.

The chapter consists of 12 units. Each unit begins with a section entitled "From inference to meaning" in which new words are introduced in meaningful contexts. Your knowledge of these new words is then reinforced through exercises, activities, and games. After every two units, you will also find a review section that goes back over the words you learned in those units. Answers to all activities are given in the Answer Key at the end of the chapter.

▌Unit 1

▌New Words

Advocate	**Hyperbole**
Bombastic	**Unassuming**
Brevity	

▌From inference to meaning

Instructions: Read the following passage and use contextual information to guess the meanings of the underlined words. Then, have a look at the table below to see how accurately you guessed the meanings.

During the trial, it became clear that the two attorneys were extremely different in style. The prosecuting attorney was loud and <u>bombastic</u>, unleashing a stream of pretentious, lengthy commentary on every topic, no matter how trivial. The defense attorney had a more <u>unassuming</u> personality, and he was a man of few words. While the prosecutor strutted around, engaging in <u>hyperbole</u> and occasionally aggravating the judge, the defense attorney was a model of <u>brevity</u>, saying no more than necessary to <u>advocate</u> for his client.

▌Your Guesses

Advocate: _____   **Hyperbole:** _____

Bombastic: _____   **Unassuming:** _____

Brevity: _____

Definitions

Advocate: argue (in support of)

Brevity: conciseness of expression

Bombastic: pompous; overblown

Hyperbole: exaggeration

Unassuming: modest

■ Word fuse

Instructions: Draw a line between each fragment in the left column and one fragment in the right column to create a word.

HY	OCATE
BOM	SUMING
ADV	PERBOLE
UNAS	VITY
BRE	BASTIC

■ Fill-ins

Instructions: Fill in the blank in each sentence below with one of the words from the following list:

advocate   bombastic   brevity   hyperbole   unassuming

1. _____ is called for in this situation, because we are running short of time.

2. Jerome wanted to become a congressman so that he could _____ for the people's interests.

3. Once you have achieved great success, the more _____ you are in your dealings with people, the more they will respect you.

4. I admit that my car isn't beautiful, but to call it the ugliest and most useless piece of machinery you've ever seen is just plain

_____.

5. During the discussion, Beverly had become so _____ that even those who supported her point of view grew weary of her speeches.

■ Word scramble

Instructions: Unscramble each of the following words. Use the hints below as needed.

1) M A G S N U U I S N _____

2) T I R E V Y B _____

3) B H O E E Y P L R _____

4) C M O T B S B A I _____

5) O A C A E V D T _____

Hints:
1) modest, 2) conciseness, 3) exaggeration, 4) pompous, 5) argue (in support of)

Matching

Instructions: Draw a line between words that have the same meaning.

hyperbole	bombastic
argue (in support of)	unassuming
pompous	advocate
conciseness	exaggeration
modest	brevity

Unit 2

New Words

Brimming	Neophyte
Disconcerting	Nugatory
Ensued	Obstreperous
Fortuitously	Officious
Morose	Ruminating

From inference to meaning

Instructions: Read the following passage and use contextual information to guess the meanings of the underlined words. Then, have a look at the table below to see how accurately you guessed the meanings.

> After almost a decade of medical school and then residential training in psychiatry, Laurel considered herself an experienced professional, but in fact she was still a <u>neophyte</u>. Her inexperience was revealed

during her first week as a staff psychiatrist at Smith Hospital. On Monday morning she entered the hospital <u>brimming</u> with confidence; by Friday evening, she exited the front door feeling so weak and <u>morose</u> she was practically ready to quit. Out of all the events that had taken place during that first week, the most deflating had been the situation involving Mr. M, an ill-tempered, <u>obstreperous</u> man who refused to cooperate with anyone under any circumstances. The fourth time Laurel had tried unsuccessfully to strike up a conversation with Mr. M, he had screamed at her and thrown a pillow at her head. She realized then that all of her precious training was essentially <u>nugatory</u>—in brief, she was unable to help the man. After that last <u>disconcerting</u> interaction with Mr. M, she forced herself to stay busy, bustling from patient to patient, reading their charts and involving herself in the details of their lives in her intense and somewhat <u>officious</u> way, but inwardly she felt discouraged. Somehow she made it through the rest of the week, but she spent most of Saturday morning sprawled on her couch, <u>ruminating</u>. <u>Fortuitously</u>, Laurel had left her jacket at the hospital. That afternoon, one of her colleagues phoned her to let her know its whereabouts. During the conversation that <u>ensued</u>, Laurel revealed how upset she was, and her colleague, who had considerably more experience, managed to reassure her.

Your Guesses

Brimming: _____   Neophyte: _____

Disconcerting: _____   Nugatory: _____

Ensued: _____   Obstreperous: _____

Fortuitously: _____   Officious: _____

Morose: _____   Ruminating: _____

Definitions

Brimming: overflowing; completely full

Disconcerting: troubling; causing uneasiness

Ensued: followed as a result

Fortuitously: by chance; fortunately

Morose: gloomy

Neophyte: beginner

Nugatory: trivial; of no value

Obstreperous: loudly defiant

Officious: intrusive; meddling

Ruminating: thinking again and again about a topic

■ Word fuse

Instructions: Draw a line between each fragment in the left column and one fragment in the right column to create a word.

FOR	ATORY
OFFI	TUITOUSLY
DISC	HYTE
NEOP	NATING
OBST	CIOUS
BRI	ONCERTING
NUG	SUED
RUMI	REPEROUS
EN	MMING

■ Fill-ins

Instructions: Fill in the blank in each sentence below with one of the words from the following list:

brimming	disconcerting	ensued	fortuitously
morose	neophyte	nugatory	obstreperous
officious	ruminating		

1. The two men argued for a long time before one shoved the other and a fistfight _____.

2. It seems rather _____ of Jack to be constantly poking his nose into Adrianna's business and telling her what to do.

3. From his _____ expression I could tell that he was depressed.

4. Sometimes I am envious of the way children wake up every morning _____ with energy.

5. You will never catch Tricia _____ about how to handle a difficult situation; rather, she acts decisively and never second-guesses herself.

6. It is not easy to negotiate a compromise with an _____ person.

7. The teacher found it somewhat _____ that his best student did so poorly on the most recent test.

8. Because nobody enforces this particular regulation, industry leaders consider it _____.

9. While driving across town, the engine of Brittany's car suddenly cut off; _____, she rolled to a stop less than 50 yards from a garage.

10. He plays guitar quite well for a _____.

Word scramble

Instructions: Unscramble each of the following words. Use the hints below as needed.

1) C I O C N T G I R N S D E _____

2) T B E S E U R O O S R P _____

3) E O O S R M _____

4) N E S E D U _____

5) T U O Y G R N A _____

6) N R U I I G A N T M _____

7) N R B I G M M I _____

8) O O C F S F U I I _____

9) T N E H O Y E P _____

10) S O O T I R T U F U _____

Hints:
1) troubling, 2) loudly defiant, 3) gloomy, 4) followed as a result, 5) trivial,
6) thinking again and again, 7) overflowing, 8) intrusive, 9) beginner, 10) by chance

Matching

Instructions: Draw a line between words that have the same meaning.

overflowing	beginner
nugatory	fortuitously
ruminating	followed as a result
loudly defiant	morose
neophyte	trivial
ensued	obstreperous
troubling	brimming
by chance	thinking again and again
officious	intrusive
gloomy	disconcerting

Review: Units 1 & 2

Contrasts

1. The adjectives "bombastic" and "unassuming" are opposed in meaning. Just as bombastic people are rarely unassuming, so unassuming people are rarely bombastic. However, the two words do not always function as complete antonyms. "Bombastic" is often used to refer to the way people express themselves in speech or in writing. A bombastic person is a person who is pompous or pretentious in expression. "Unassuming" refers in a more general way to a person's character or personality. Unassuming people are modest, perhaps even shy, and unlikely to be bombastic when they express themselves.

2. Key vocabulary words can be confused with each other when they differ in just one sound. For example, consider the words "morose" and "morass." "Morose" is an adjective that means "sad" or "gloomy." As discussed in Unit 4 of Chapter 1, "morass" is a noun that refers to a marsh or a swamp or a complicated, confusing or troublesome situation.

Fast facts

1. The adjectival form of "brevity" is "brief." Someone who can be brief in his or her remarks is demonstrating brevity. However, as a noun, a "brief" is a legal document that summarizes a client's case. As a verb, to "brief" someone means to give them essential information. If you ask an attorney to briefly brief you on a brief, you are asking for a quick summary of a legal case.

2. The word "officious" stems from the Latin word "officium," which means duty. This Latin root appears in English words such as "office," "officer," and "official." However, the meanings of these words are neutral, while "officious" means to do one's duty to the point of being meddlesome.

■ Grammar stretches

Instructions: Fill in the blank in each sentence below with one of the words from the following list. You may have to change the grammatical form of each word in order for it to fit into a sentence.

advocate   brimming   disconcerting   ensued   fortuitously
morose   neophyte   obstreperous   officious   ruminating
unassuming

1. After waiting in line for several hours, the fans rushed into the stadium when the gates opened, and many people got shoved around or stepped on in the _____ chaos.

2. "Since I got laid off," Martin whispered _____, "I've been feeling too unhappy to look for another job."

3. How _____ that Professor Jones canceled class on the very day I was too sick to attend!

4. The poorest citizens of their country lack political power because no one has _____ effectively for their interests.

5. Following the interview, Ariel _____ for several hours about her performance, imagining the various answers she could have made to the interviewer's questions.

6. Whenever Brad's Aunt visited him, she would snoop around his apartment, ask him personal questions, offer detailed advice on virtually every topic, and otherwise aggravate him with her _____.

7. It _____ me to look into the mirror each morning and see the gray hairs gradually crowding out the darker ones.

8. Riley was a shy child who spoke quietly and _____, and rarely caused her teachers any trouble.

9. The _____ in our group need to be a little more respectful of the old-timers, in my opinion.

10. As Mr. Matthews grew more ill, his natural _____ increased, and he became less and less willing to cooperate with the nurses.

11. He spoke of his younger daughter in a voice that _____ with affection and pride.

■ Error watch

Instructions: In the following sentences, note whether the underlined word is used correctly or not. Circle the **C** at the end of the sentence if the word is used correctly; circle the **I** if it is used incorrectly.

1. If you continue to speak with such <u>brevity</u>, your audience will lose interest; keep your speeches short!   C   I

2. Joe claims that on this particular stretch of road the speed limit is <u>nugatory</u>, because it's never enforced by the police.   C   I

3. The congressman has an undistinguished record thus far; it seems like cheap <u>hyperbole</u> to compare him to Abraham Lincoln.   C   I

4. Following the accident, the two drivers stood toe-to-toe, shouting at each other <u>fortuitously</u>.   C   I

5. He shook his head <u>bombastically</u>, saddened by the comment his uncle had just made.   C   I

6. Jolene was quite <u>disconcerted</u> to discover a leak in her roof.   C   I

■ Matching

Instructions: Draw a line between words that have the same meaning.

intrusive	trivial
obstreperous	unassuming
nugatory	morose
pompous	advocate
overflowing	brevity
conciseness	bombastic
exaggeration	beginner
thinking again and again	followed as a result
fortuitously	hyperbole
troubling	officious
modest	brimming
ensued	ruminating
gloomy	disconcerting
argue (in support of)	by chance
neophyte	loudly defiant

Unit 3

New Words

Autonomous

Equanimity

Mollify

Petulant

Propensity

Tractable

From inference to meaning

Instructions: Read the following passage and use contextual information to guess the meanings of the underlined words. Then, have a look at the table below to see how accurately you guessed the meanings.

Although Cecilia was a sweet and cooperative child, she was not excessively <u>tractable</u>, according to her father. Rather, she was quite independent and capable of speaking up for herself. She had a <u>propensity</u> for making decisions on her own, but her father was pleased to find that in spite of her <u>autonomous</u> nature, she typically consulted with him before carrying out her plans. She was also a very patient child. While some children are <u>petulant</u>, irritated by the slightest problem or challenge, Cecilia showed a remarkable <u>equanimity</u> at all times, even in difficult circumstances. And when she became angry or frustrated, as all children do sometimes, it was relatively easy to <u>mollify</u> her.

Your Guesses

Autonomous: _____

Equanimity: _____

Mollify: _____

Petulant: _____

Propensity: _____

Tractable: _____

Definitions

Autonomous: independent; self-governed

Equanimity: even-temperedness; calmness

Mollify: soothe; pacify

Petulant: irritable; rude

Propensity: tendency

Tractable: easily managed or controlled

Word fuse

Instructions: Draw a line between each fragment in the left column and one fragment in the right column to create a word.

PRO	NIMITY
MOL	TONOMOUS
AU	PENSITY
PET	LIFY
TRA	ULANT
EQUA	CTABLE

■ Fill-ins

Instructions: Fill in the blank in each sentence below with one of the words from the following list:

> autonomous   equanimity   mollify   petulant   propensity
> tractable

1. The more we talked, the more we got on each other's nerves; I have to admit that we were both awfully _____.

2. People who are at complete peace with themselves can face the world with complete _____.

3. Jada has a _____ to overthink her homework assignments.

4. Agency leaders hope to function in a more _____ way once the new legislation is passed, rather than continuing to rely on each other for support.

5. Because Henry was so _____, his boss often took advantage of him.

6. No matter how hard I tried, I was unable to _____ the angry woman.

▪ Word scramble

Instructions: Unscramble each of the following words. Use the hints below as needed.

1) Y O P I P E T N R S _____

2) S T A N O O O U M U _____

3) O Y L F M L I _____

4) E T C A A T L B R _____

5) N Q M T E I A U Y I _____

6) T U P N L T E A _____

Hints:
1) tendency, 2) independent, 3) soothe, 4) easily managed, 5) even-temperedness,
6) irritable

▪ Matching

Instructions: Draw a line between words that have the same meaning.

soothe	independent
autonomous	irritable
even-temperedness	mollify
petulant	tendency
tractable	equanimity
propensity	easily managed

Unit 4

New Words

Fatuous	Minatory
Forestall	Obviate
Gouge	Quibbles
Lucidity	Refractory
Ludicrous	Subsided

From inference to meaning

Instructions: Read the following passage and use contextual information to guess the meanings of the underlined words. Then, have a look at the table below to see how accurately you guessed the meanings.

In spite of the man's <u>fatuous</u> expression, I had to take him and his complaint seriously. I was the only salesperson in the store at the moment, and part of my job was to address the various <u>quibbles</u> and concerns that customers periodically brought to us. "Your company tried to <u>gouge</u> me," the man was saying, "charging so much for a computer that doesn't work right. You didn't tell me I had to install the software. You didn't tell me I had to pay for Internet service...." At that point I interrupted him, hoping to <u>forestall</u> any unpleasantness. Clearly the man knew very little about computers. I began to explain, but after a few moments his eyes glazed over. Gripping the counter with both hands, a <u>minatory</u> expression crossing his face, the man began threatening to sue me and my company. Again, I found myself struggling to take him seriously, with his <u>ludicrous</u> talk of lawsuits, his bright yellow shirt, and the <u>refractory</u> little patch of hair on one side of his head that refused to lie flat. The man was practically shouting now, and his comments had lost most of their <u>lucidity</u>. "Alright," I said, trying to <u>obviate</u> the need for calling the police, "you're right. You're absolutely right. Let's talk about what we can do for you." My plan now was to stall for time until his anger <u>subsided</u> and I could attempt once again to reason with him.

Your Guesses

Fatuous: _____   Minatory: _____

Forestall: _____   Obviate: _____

Gouge: _____   Quibbles: _____

Lucidity: _____   Refractory: _____

Ludicrous: _____   Subsided: _____

Definitions

Fatuous: foolish

Forestall: prevent; ward off

Gouge: cheat; extort

Lucidity: clarity

Ludicrous: ridiculous; absurd and laughable

Minatory: threatening

Obviate: make unnecessary

Quibbles: trivial complaints or objections

Refractory: stubborn; unresponsibe

Subsided: diminished; abated

Word fuse

Instructions: Draw a line between each fragment in the left column and one fragment in the right column to create a word.

REF	ESTALL
MINA	BBLES
FAT	UOUS
SUB	IDITY
GO	RACTORY
FOR	ICROUS
OB	SIDED
LUC	TORY
QUI	VIATE
LUD	UGE

■ Fill-ins

Instructions: Fill in the blank in each sentence below with one of the words from the following list:

fatuous	forestall	gouge	lucidity	ludicrous
minatory	obviate	quibbles	refractory	subsided

1. The president's economic advisors held an emergency meeting to discuss how to _____ the country's imminent financial crisis.

2. Like a _____ child, the patient refused to take his medicine.

3. Lonnie has never stolen anything in his entire life; the allegation that he took Rosalind's purse is completely _____.

4. With a _____ smile, the student walked up to the blackboard and proceeded to write down the wrong answer to the teacher's question.

5. As the committee worked together on a draft of the document, there were numerous _____ about minor details of the wording.

6. Because of his great size, a scowling expression, and the prominent scar on one cheek, John had a rather _____ appearance.

7. Once the floodwaters had _____, the engineers were able to evaluate the extent of the damage.

8. Wearing a helmet while riding a bicycle can _____ the risk of injury.

9. Watkins' argument before the high court was remarkable for both its passion as well as its _____.

10. This particular corporation has a nasty tendency to _____ its clients at every opportunity.

Word scramble

Instructions: Unscramble each of the following words. Use the hints below as needed.

1) D I L C Y T I U _____

2) B Q S E L I B U _____

3) E V I O A B T _____

4) L O T R L E F A S _____

5) Y E F T R O A C R R _____

6) C L S R D I U O U _____

7) A I M O T N Y R _____

8) E U O G G _____

9) U A O S F U T _____

10) E S D U B D I S _____

Hints:
1) clarity, 2) trivial complaints, 3) make unnecessary, 4) prevent, 5) stubborn, 6) ridiculous, 7) threatening, 8) cheat, 9) foolish, 10) diminished

■ Matching

Instructions: Draw a line between words that have the same meaning.

gouge	quibbles
trivial complaints	refractory
obviate	clarity
diminished	ridiculous
fatuous	cheat
stubborn	subsided
forestall	minatory
lucidity	make unnecessary
threatening	foolish
ludicrous	prevent

Review: Units 3 & 4

Contrasts

1. Key vocabulary words can be confused with each other when they differ in just one sound. For example, consider the verbs "gouge" and "gauge." As used in Unit 4, "gouge" means to extort or cheat. (It also means to cut or to dig out with a thumb.) "Gauge" means to estimate. For example, an emergency medical technician who is examining an injured person may need to *gauge* the size of a *gouge* in the person's arm.

2. The verb "mollify" is synonymous with "assuage" (see Unit 2 of Chapter 1, as well as the Review for Units 5 and 6 of that chapter).

3. "Ludicrous" and "fatuous" are somewhat similar in meaning, but "ludicrous" refers to anything that provokes ridicule or derision, while "fatuous" refers to actions and statements that appear foolish and self-satisfied. For example:

   The councilman's proposal to repave all of the roads in the city within a one-year period is *ludicrous*. "We can do this," he said to the council *fatuously*.

Fast facts

1. The adjective "minatory" comes from the Latin word "minari," meaning "to threaten." This Latin root can also be seen in the English words "menace" and "menacing."

2. The word "propensity" comes from a combination of the Latin words "pro" (forward) and "pendere" (hang). A propensity is a tendency to do something. If you have a propensity for eating chips, then your desire for chips is, so to speak, hanging forward and pulling you toward them. The Latin root "pendere" can also be seen in other English words as well. A "pendant" is a hanging object, such as a piece of jewelry attached to a necklace. A "pendulous" object is one that is hanging or drooping. When we say that an issue is "pending," we mean that it is not yet decided—it is

still hanging in the air, so to speak. And when we "append" something, we are attaching it to (i.e., hanging it on) something else. For example:

Alicia had a *propensity* for wearing expensive jewelry. One day, as she wandered through an antique store, a large *pendant* caught her eye. It was a jade elephant that hung *pendulously* from a thin gold necklace. Alicia asked the store owner about the price; he replied that another customer wanted to purchase it, and that the sale was *pending*.

■ Fill-ins

Instructions: Fill in the blank in each sentence below with one of the words from the following list:

> equanimity   ludicrous   gouge   minatory   propensity
> tractable

1. Our pricing structure varies from project to project, but our company would never _____ a client.

2. The invading army was a dark and _____ presence in the daily lives of the villagers.

3. Matthias was a great leader because he handled all situations, whether urgent, frightening, or complex, with the same _____ and poise.

4. I believe that the conflict in our schedules is _____ and thus easily remedied.

5. My father was raised in a conservative household, and so he considers tattoos, piercings, and other forms of body art to be _____.

6. Being such a generous woman, Martha had a _____ to donate to every charitable organization that approached her.

■ Grammar stretches

Instructions: Fill in the blank in each sentence below with one of the words from the following list. You may have to change the grammatical form of each word in order for it to fit into a sentence.

autonomous	fatuous	forestall	lucidity	mollify
obviate	petulant	quibbles	refractory	subsided

1. Once Robbie loses his temper, very little can be done by way of _____ him.

2. Given the extent of her _____, it is no surprise that their foreign minister refused to renegotiate our original trade agreement.

3. The social studies teacher was impressed by how clearly organized and _____ Tim's paper turned out to be.

4. Liz was capable of exceptional _____, pouting and complaining whenever someone disagreed with her or failed to do things her way.

5. Although his wife was gravely ill, Gerald continued to be preoccupied with improving his golf game, reducing his waistline, and otherwise behaving _____.

6. Our disagreement about the third item of the contract is merely a _____ rather than representing a fundamental difference.

7. Instead of consulting with the manager every time you make a personnel-related decision, we would like you to handle your decision-making more _____.

8. Prior to describing the new semiconductor technology, the engineering professor made some comments to the class that _____ any confusion about what would be covered on the next test.

9. Not until her anger _____ will Francine be able to approach her brother about his indiscretions.

10. He used to think that brushing and flossing one's teeth regularly _____ the need for regular visits to the dentist.

Error watch

Instructions: In the following sentences, note whether the underlined word is used correctly or not. Circle the C at the end of the sentence if the word is used correctly; circle the I if it is used incorrectly.

1. I wish my younger son were more cooperative instead of being so <u>minatory</u> about every little detail and doing things his own way.   C   I

2. Sheila met every crisis with admirable <u>equanimity</u> and poise.   C   I

3. By treating the wound yourself, you will <u>mollify</u> the need for a doctor.   C   I

4. It is <u>obviate</u> that Rita loves algebra.   C   I

5. Farley is not a <u>refractory</u> person, even though he has strong opinions and is quite capable of standing up for them.   C   I

■ Matching

Instructions: Draw a line between words that have the same meaning.

minatory	propensity
prevent	gouge
ludicrous	soothe
foolish	irritable
tendency	trivial complaints
obviate	threatening
petulant	even-temperedness
lucidity	independent
cheat	subsided
easily managed	refractory
diminished	clarity
mollify	make unnecessary
quibbles	fatuous
stubborn	forestall
autonomous	ridiculous
equanimity	tractable

Unit 5

New Words

Chagrin   Stammered

Furtively   Vacated

Protracting

From inference to meaning

Instructions: Read the following excerpt from "Outcasts in Salt Lake City," by James Weldon Johnson, and use contextual information to guess the meanings of the underlined words. Then, have a look at the table below to see how accurately you guessed the meanings.

> The clerk was busy at the key-rack. He glanced at us <u>furtively</u>, but kept himself occupied. It grew obvious that he was <u>protracting</u> his time. Finally, he could delay no longer and came to the desk. As he came his expression revealed the lie he was to speak. He turned the register around, examined our names, and while his face flushed a bit said, "I'm sorry, but we haven't got a vacant room." This statement, which I knew almost absolutely to be false, set a number of emotions in action: humiliation, <u>chagrin</u>, indignation, resentment, anger; but in the midst of them all I could detect a sense of pity for the man who had to make it, for he was, to all appearances, an honest, decent person. It was then about eleven o'clock, and I sought the eyes of the clerk and asked if he expected any rooms to be <u>vacated</u> at noon. He <u>stammered</u> that he did not ...

Your Guesses

Chagrin: _____   Stammered: _____

Furtively: _____   Vacated: _____

Protracting: _____

Definitions

Chagrin: emotional distress due to error or failure

Furtively: secretly; evasively

Protracting: lengthening

Stammered: spoke haltingly, with unintended pauses and repetitions

Vacated: left; emptied

Word fuse

Instructions: Draw a line between each fragment in the left column and one fragment in the right column to create a word.

FUR	CATED
VA	RACTING
ST	TIVELY
CHA	AMMERED
PROT	GRIN

Fill-ins

Instructions: Fill in the blank in each sentence below with one of the words from the following list:

chagrin   furtively   protracting   stammered   vacated

1. If you listen to the tape closely, you can hear Tammy and Cyndi whispering _____ in the background.

2. Once the tenants had _____ the apartment, the landlord was able to replace the carpeting.

3. The two committee members kept on quibbling over a trivial point, thereby _____ the meeting.

4. Much to her _____, Melissa realized that her comment had deeply offended their host.

5. The witness was clearly intimidated by the atmosphere of the courtroom and consequently _____ through most of his testimony.

■ Word scramble

Instructions: Unscramble each of the following words. Use the hints below as needed.

1) A S R E M D T E M _____

2) R H G C N I A _____

3) D E C V T A A _____

4) N C O T I R R G A P T _____

5) L T U I F V Y E R _____

Hints:
1) spoke haltingly, 2) distress due to error or failure, 3) left, 4) lengthening, 5) secretly

Matching

Instructions: Draw a line between words that have the same meaning.

lengthening	distress due to error or failure
secretly	protracting
chagrin	left
vacated	stammered
spoke haltingly	furtively

Unit 6

New Words

Cognizant	Resilient
Despondent	Stymied
Divulged	Vacillated
Entails	Vicariously
Goad	Welter
Proclaimed	

From inference to meaning

Instructions: Read the following passage and use contextual information to guess the meanings of the underlined words. Then, have a look at the table below to see how accurately you guessed the meanings.

Not long before the Jackson family's annual camping trip, Hal Jackson slipped on a patch of ice and sprained his ankle. Hal concealed the injury from his family and tried to take care of it himself, but his efforts were <u>stymied</u> by the fact that he was a construction worker and had to be on his feet all day. Soon he became <u>cognizant</u> of the fact that the ankle was seriously damaged and wouldn't heal in time for the trip. He <u>divulged</u> the details of his injury at a family dinner two days before they were scheduled to leave, then he announced that, regretfully, he would not be able to join them this year. "You old sissy," exclaimed one of his brothers, trying to <u>goad</u> Hal into changing his mind, "have you gone soft on us?" Hal <u>vacillated</u> for a few moments, wondering if he might be able to manage. Then he remembered what a Jackson family camping trip <u>entails</u>: long hikes, rock climbing, and endless football games with a <u>welter</u> of cousins and nephews. "Can't do it," he <u>proclaimed</u>. "Just call me every night and tell me what you did; I'll enjoy it <u>vicariously</u>." The family was disappointed but by no means <u>despondent</u>; they knew Hal was a <u>resilient</u> man who would heal soon and join them on the trip the following year.

Your Guesses

Cognizant: _____   Resilient: _____

Despondent: _____   Stymied: _____

Divulged: _____   Vacillated: _____

Entails: _____   Vicariously: _____

Goad: _____   Welter: _____

Proclaimed: _____

Definitions

Cognizant: aware

Despondent: without hope

Divulged: revealed secret or private information

Entails: requires; logically implies

Goad: provoke; prod

Proclaimed: announced; formally declared

Resilient: capable of recovering easily

Stymied: thwarted; blocked

Vacillated: shifted indecisively

Vicariously: secondhand; indirectly

Welter: disorderly mix; clutter

■ Word fuse

Instructions: Draw a line between each fragment in the left column and one fragment in the right column to create a word

RES	MIED
VI	CLAIMED
GO	ULGED
DIV	ONDENT
WE	NIZANT
STY	AD
EN	ILLATED
PRO	ILIENT
DESP	TAILS
VAC	LTER
COG	CARIOUSLY

■ Fill-ins

Instructions: Fill in the blank in each sentence below with one of the words from the following list:

cognizant	despondent	divulged	entails	goad
proclaimed	resilient	stymied	vacillated	vicariously
welter				

1. They _____ too long and the opportunity was lost.

2. After failing three classes last semester, Blake became _____ and decided to drop out of college.

3. Today the leaders of the two countries _____ that a new era of peace between them had arrived.

4. If you continue to _____ Darla with complaints about her attitude, she is likely to respond by becoming even less cooperative.

5. Phil was deeply involved in every aspect of his son's life, and his mood was closely linked to his son's successes and failures; many people thought that Phil was living _____ through the boy.

6. The neurosurgeon began the delicate process of removing the tumor, fully _____ of the fact that that the slightest mistake could cause further damage.

7. Abe's desk was a _____ of books, articles, and papers, along with photographs of his three children, an ashtray or two, and the occasional soda can.

8. Because she is so _____, I'm sure Debbie will overcome this latest setback.

9. Jim's wife wanted to know exactly how much information he had _____ to friends about their last quarrel.

10. Efforts by the two senators to gather support for their tax reform bill were _____ by a lack of public support for the bill.

11. Being the accountant for this particular company _____ more than the usual range of responsibilities.

■ Word scramble

Instructions: Unscramble each of the following words. Use the hints below as needed.

1) U I L D E G V _____

2) T E M S D I Y _____

3) E E W R T L _____

4) A I G N C T Z N O _____

5) L S R T E I I N E _____

6) S A O I Y R C L I V U _____

7) A D O G _____

8) N E O E D P S N T D _____

9) R P C O A D L E I M _____

10) E I L D C L A V T A _____

11) L T I S N A E _____

Hints:
1) revealed secret, 2) thwarted, 3) disorderly mix, 4) aware, 5) recovers easily, 6) secondhand, 7) provoke, 8) without hope, 9) announced, 10) shifted indecisively, 11) requires

■ Matching

Instructions: Draw a line between words that have the same meaning.

provoke	secondhand
resilient	cognizant
welter	proclaimed
without hope	goad
aware	divulged
vacillated	entails
announced	recovers easily
requires	thwarted
vicariously	despondent
revealed secret	shifted indecisively
stymied	disorderly mix

Review: Units 5 & 6

Fast facts

1. The word "vacated" comes the Latin word for "empty"—to vacate is to voluntarily remove oneself and one's possessions from a place, or to voluntary resign from a position. The end result is that the place or position will be empty. For example, we can say that at some point after an executive has told her boss that she is vacating her position (i.e., resigning), she will need to vacate her office.

   Related words in English include "vacancy" and "vacuum." We can describe an empty or unoccupied space as "vacant," and when we say that a person has a "vacant" look, we mean that their expression is empty or distant. When we go on "vacation," we leave our workplace empty, so to speak. And a "vacuous" idea or person is one that is "empty" of intelligence.

2. The word "cognizant" comes from the Latin words "com" (together) and "gnoscere" (to know). The word "gnoscere" appears in many other English words, such as "cognition" and "recognition." The "cognoscenti" are people who are especially well-informed about a particular topic. And the military term "reconnaissance" refers to a search for useful information. The verb form for reconnaissance is "reconnoiter." For example:

   The purpose of the soldier's *reconnaissance* of the valley was to determine the strength of the enemy forces. Once he had finished *reconnoitering* the area, he returned to his squad.

■ Grammar stretches

Instructions: Fill in the blank in each sentence below with one of the words from the following list. You may have to change the grammatical form of each word in order for it to fit into a sentence.

cognizant	despondent	divulged	entails	furtively
goad	proclaimed	protracting	resilient	stammered
stymied	vacated	vacillated	vicariously	

1. Once the priest finished his sermon, there was a _____ silence while the congregation pondered the meaning of what he had said.

2. The steepness of the south face of the mountain _____ any attempt to climb it.

3. Once the anesthesia began to take effect, I lost all _____ of my surroundings.

4. Lee always took _____ pleasure at seeing his daughter enjoy the zoo.

5. Because Jason has a crush on Lizbeth, he often sneaks _____ glances at her during class.

6. The fact that Carla has survived two open-heart surgeries and is now leading a productive life demonstrates her exceptional _____.

7. "I hate my new glasses," said the child _____. "Now I'll never be a pilot when I grow up."

8. Kylie's boss is so intimidating that most of her colleagues end up _____ whenever they speak to him.

9. My best friend and I were both _____ about whether to go to Miami or to Key West for spring break.

10. After being _____ by his wife for years to get into shape, Louis finally joined a local gym and began working out.

11. The staff sergeant was arrested for _____ military secrets to non-military personnel.

12. The eviction notice stated that the man must _____ the building immediately.

13. In the movie, the hero stands on a car to loudly _____ his love for his girlfriend.

14. Asking my mother for money used to _____ hearing a speech from her about the importance of financial planning.

■ Error watch

Instructions: In the following sentences, note whether the underlined word is used correctly or not. Circle the C at the end of the sentence if the word is used correctly; circle the I if it is used incorrectly.

1. Leena could barely walk into her room due to the <u>welter</u> of clothes, books, and guitars that seemed to fill every available space.   C   I

2. My sister is so <u>vicarious</u>; she has the hardest time making up her mind.   C   I

3. The realization that she had spent almost a decade attempting to salvage a marriage that was ultimately doomed filled her with <u>chagrin</u>.   C   I

4. The organization's plans to register new voters were repeatedly <u>divulged</u> by logistical challenges.   C   I

5. After a <u>protracted</u> illness, Nima's poodle finally recovered.   C   I

6. I am not <u>cognizant</u> of any objection to the advice of this committee.   C   I

■ Matching

Instructions: Draw a line between words that have the same meaning.

lengthening	secretly
entails	goad
provoke	vicariously
recovers easily	left
vacated	vacillated
secondhand	protracting
despondent	resilient
furtively	proclaim
distress due to error or failure	chagrin
welter	stymied
shifted indecisively	spoke haltingly
cognizant	disorderly mix
revealed secret	divulged
thwarted	aware
announce	without hope
stammered	requires

■ Word Search

Instructions: All of the new words from Units 5 and 6 are hidden in this challenging puzzle. The words may be written forwards or backwards in any direction: horizontal, vertical, or diagonal. Some words overlap in one letter. Your task is to circle each word as you have found it.

Following are the meanings of the words you're looking for. (Remember: You're searching for the actual words, not the meanings given here.)

spoke haltingly	left	distress due to error or failure
lengthening	secretly	revealed secret
thwarted	disorderly mix	aware
recovers easily	secondhand	provoke
without hope	announced	shifted indecisively
requires		

```
C P E R M S H O E F D E M I A L C O R P
O R A D E S P O N D E N T S L O W L O O
G A S O L S C R A I P O W H I R E A S L
N T L D E O I I M S D E I M Y T S A V E
I A X O E R S L Y U N X L Y W O T U M E
Z E A B R K E V I N O G L J E D E V H N
A V N L U N Y I M E M N I E V E A E I R
N A W M T O P I R F N I S U A B N P W R
T C L A R A L D E O S T A M M E R E D O
M I I T E L I N G S D C H N E E L A J E
E L L F N V H O R T E A M E I T E E N N
S L T Q U A R A L G R R O R E L G O A D
I A U L N R E V O M I T A R M E A D L E
E T G S E P T I S D M O L U A S C L O T
T E E D S Z Y I M O P R Q U S R T U Y A
D D A R A O M T V R S P O N I R G A H C
R O B E W K A N C E Y G U G K E A L A A
E T S U E T H S T E L L V U A I W L I V
M V I C A R I O U S L Y E K N A G E L O
```

Unit 7

New Words

Autocratic   Sentient

Coerced   Sublime

Pageant

From inference to meaning

Instructions: Read the following excerpt from Albert Einstein's essay "The World as I See It" and guess the meanings of the underlined words. Then, have a look at the table below to see how accurately you guessed the meanings.

> I am quite aware that for any organization to reach its goals, one man must do the thinking and directing and generally bear the responsibility. But the led must not be <u>coerced</u>, they must be able to choose their leader. In my opinion, an <u>autocratic</u> system of coercion soon degenerates; force attracts men of low morality. . . . The really valuable thing in the <u>pageant</u> of human life seems to me not the political state, but the creative, <u>sentient</u> individual, the personality; it alone creates the noble and the <u>sublime</u>, while the herd as such remains dull in thought and dull in feeling.

Your Guesses

Autocratic: _____   Sentient: _____

Coerced: _____   Sublime: _____

Pageant: _____

Definitions

Autocratic: excessively controlling

Coerced: forced

Pageant: elaborate public display

Sentient: conscious; able to perceive

Sublime: awe-inspiring; exalted

Word fuse

Instructions: Draw a line between each fragment in the left column and one fragment in the right column to create a word.

SEN	LIME
COE	TIENT
SUB	EANT
AUTO	CRATIC
PAG	RCED

Fill-ins

Instructions: Fill in the blank in each sentence below with one of the words from the following list:

autocratic   coerced   pageant   sentient   sublime

1. The third graders at Kelley's school put on a delightful _____ to celebrate the arrival of spring.

2. Our trip to southern Italy last summer was absolutely _____.

3. Did the soldiers volunteer for this assignment, or were they _____ by their commanding officer?

4. Bill was an avid astronomer and science-fiction buff who hoped that someday _____ beings would be discovered on some distant planet.

5. Even at home, the executive exhibited a disturbingly _____ personality; at all times he expected compliance from his wife and obedience from his children.

■ Word scramble

Instructions: Unscramble each of the following words. Use the hints below as needed.

1) B E S I U M L _____

2) T T S I N N E E _____

3) R U C I T A C T A O _____

4) N G E A T P A _____

5) D R C E O E C _____

Hints:
1) awe-inspiring, 2) conscious, 3) excessively controlling, 4) elaborate public display, 5) forced

Matching

Instructions: Draw a line between words that have the same meaning.

pageant   sentient

excessively controlling   coerced

sublime   elaborate public display

forced   awe-inspiring

conscious   autocratic

Unit 8

New Words

Entreated	Nascent
Gaudy	Nomenclature
Hiatus	Oblivious
Histrionics	Tenacious
Inconspicuous	Traversing
Indigenous	

From inference to meaning

Instructions: Read the following passage and use contextual information to guess the meanings of the underlined words. Then, have a look at the table below to see how accurately you guessed the meanings.

Ever since he was a little boy, Harold had been fascinated by butterflies. While most of us could pass an entire day at the park or in a wooded area largely <u>oblivious</u> to all but the largest and most <u>gaudy</u> specimens, Harold noticed every butterfly he encountered, no matter how <u>inconspicuous</u>. By the time he was 6, he had developed his own <u>nomenclature</u> for identifying different species; by age 10, he had read numerous books and had mastered the scientific terminology. His <u>nascent</u> expertise quickly deepened, and by his sophomore year at Princeton he had already published three scientific papers on the feeding patterns of a local species. It was at this point that he decided to take a year off to do field work in Arkansas. His mother strongly objected to the <u>hiatus</u>. "If you leave school now," she complained, "you may never go back." At times she was forceful, demanding that he give up his plan; an hour later she would be fighting back tears as she <u>entreated</u> him to reconsider. Harold ignored her <u>histrionics</u>. He was determined to spend the year <u>traversing</u> the countryside of Arkansas, studying the <u>indigenous</u> species as well as those that passed through the state during their annual migration He knew that if he were sufficiently <u>tenacious</u>, he would wear his mother down until she relented.

Your Guesses

Entreated: _____   Nascent: _____

Gaudy: _____   Nomenclature: _____

Hiatus: _____   Oblivious: _____

Histrionics: _____   Tenacious: _____

Inconspicuous: _____   Traversing: _____

Indigenous: _____

Definitions

Entreated: requested urgently

Gaudy: tastelessly showy

Hiatus: temporary break; gap

Histrionics: overly dramatic and emotional behavior

Inconspicuous: not readily noticed

Indigenous: native

Nascent: emerging; coming into being

Nomenclature: a set of names and rules for naming

Oblivious: unmindful; unaware

Tenacious: persistent; holding fast

Traversing: traveling across

◼ Word fuse

Instructions: Draw a line between each fragment in the left column and one fragment in the right column to create a word.

INC	UDY
OB	NCLATURE
TRA	LIVIOUS
HIA	CIOUS
NOME	TUS
EN	CENT
IN	ONSPICUOUS
TENA	TRIONICS
HIS	TREATED
NAS	VERSING
GA	DIGENOUS

■ Fill-ins

Instructions: Fill in the blank in each sentence below with one of the words from the following list:

entreated	gaudy	hiatus	histrionics
inconspicuous	indigenous	nascent	nomenclature
oblivious	tenacious	traversing	

1. Jean is taking a little _____ from work this week in order to attend to some personal matters.

2. It amazes me sometimes how _____ my young son can be to the fact that one of his shoelaces is untied, or that he has peanut butter smeared on his pants, or that he has put his shirt on backwards.

3. Having learned the _____ for describing the various types of beer, Ralph enjoyed showing off his newfound knowledge to his friends.

4. An experienced spy knows how to be present and yet _____.

5. Carly's diamond-encrusted pendant is one of the largest and most _____ pieces of jewelry I have seen in years.

6. If you are sufficiently _____, you can achieve almost anything.

7. The Yanomamo are an _____ people who live in the upper Amazon region of South America.

8. Last year Marquis started his own consulting firm; he worked long hours at first as he sought to attract clients to his _____ business.

9. Although as a child he had been bitten by a rattlesnake there, Dan's fondness for _____ the Arizona desert was as strong as it had ever been.

10. A hint of desperation crept into her voice as Janet _____ the ticket agent to sell her a seat on the next flight.

11. I wasn't impressed by the actor's _____; I felt that he exaggerated his character's inner torment to the point of caricature.

■ Word scramble

Instructions: Unscramble each of the following words. Use the hints below as needed.

1) U E I T N O C S A _____

2) P O I S I U N N C U C S O _____

3) I N S R S O I C H T I _____

4) A E T N N C S _____

5) A N R T E T D E E _____

6) R C N T M A E U N E L O _____

7) T H A S U I _____

8) I V S R A N R E G T _____

9) S U B V O L O I I _____

10) Y U G D A _____

11) N S G I N U D E O I _____

Hints:
1) persistent, 2) not readily noticed, 3) overly dramatic behavior, 4) emerging,
5) requested urgently, 6) a set of names, 7) temporary break, 8) traveling across,
9) unmindful, 10) tastelessly showy, 11) native

Matching

Instructions: Draw a line between words that have the same meaning.

a set of names	native
indigenous	traveling across
entreated	not readily noticed
unmindful	nomenclature
nascent	overly dramatic behavior
traversing	temporary break
persistent	oblivious
inconspicuous	gaudy
hiatus	requested urgently
tastelessly showy	tenacious
histrionics	emerging

Review: Units 7 & 8

Contrasts

1. The adjectives "sentient" and "cognizant" (Unit 6) both refer to conscious awareness. However, "sentient" refers to the general capacity for awareness. "Cognizant" refers to awareness of something in particular. For example:

> Jerry believes that plants are *sentient* beings. He talks to his plants, because he thinks they are *cognizant* on some level of what he is saying.

2. The adjective "tenacious" is similar in meaning to the adjective "resolute" (see Reviews for Units 3 & 4 and Units 9 & 10 in Chapter 1). Both terms indicate firmness of belief. However, "tenacious" implies firmness to an extreme—a person who is tenacious just won't let go—and the term applies to behaviors as well as beliefs. A person who is described as "resolute" is simply firm in his or her particular beliefs.

Fast facts

1. The verb "traversing" comes from the Latin words "trans" (across) and "vertere" (turn). Thus, the term means to travel across a particular place. A related term, the adjective "transverse," refers to the arrangement of one thing crosswise to another, as in the relationship between the horizontal stroke in the letter "t" and the vertical stroke.

2. The adjective "nascent" comes from the Latin word "nasci," which means "born." Thus, a "renaissance" is a sort of revival or rebirth. Other words that originate from "nasci" include "natal" (related to birth) and "innate" (present at birth). For example:

> Babies have many *innate* characteristics that are not apparent until the *postnatal* period, when they can be readily observed.

Fill-ins

Instructions: Fill in the blank in each sentence below with one of the words from the following list.

autocracy   hiatus   nascent   nomenclature   sublime

1. Cecilia is an extraordinarily talented violist; her playing is
_____.

2. What _____ should we use to label the different elements of a professional organization?

3. Following a _____ of more than a decade, Dr. Wang decided to return to academia.

4. Although officially a democracy, the government of this country functions more like an _____.

5. After studying German for a year, Alex spent a summer in Berlin in order to improve upon his _____ skills.

Grammar stretches

Instructions: Fill in the blank in each sentence below with one of the words from the following list. You may have to change the grammatical form of each word in order for it to fit into a sentence.

coerced   entreated   gaudy   histrionics   inconspicuous
indigenous   oblivious   pageant   sentient   tenacious
traversing

1. Although Hector is famous, his small size and tendency to wear sunglasses and ordinary clothing allow him to wander the streets
_____.

2. The police officer was found guilty of _____ the suspect to sign a confession.

3. Some people believe that only human beings are capable of
_____; however, I think it's clear that animals are conscious,
and that they have the capacity to reflect on themselves and their
surroundings.

4. Both cars are extraordinary, but the bright purple Cadillac with gold
trim is definitely the _____ of the two.

5. Someday Lillian hopes to _____ the Australian outback
with her older brothers.

6. The more Peter ignored her, the more _____ Patricia registered her dissatisfaction, with heavy sighs, pointed looks, and melodramatic remarks.

7. The child dug into his ice cream with such _____ that
within seconds the bowl was empty.

8. Such _____! How could you forget the two things I asked
you to buy at the grocery store?

9. The giant panda is _____ to western China.

10. Carmen believed that if she kept on _____ her boss to let
her take an extra week off in June, her boss would eventually agree to
the plan.

11. Denzel loves the _____ of the New Year's Day parade in
our city.

■ Error watch

Instructions: In the following sentences, note whether the underlined word is used correctly or not. Circle the C at the end of the sentence if the word is used correctly; circle the I if it is used incorrectly.

1. Good thing Mike was so <u>oblivious</u>; otherwise he would have never convinced his teacher to give him an extension on the term paper.   C   I

2. It would be better for you to remain <u>indigenous</u> rather than allowing the two men to see you.   C   I

3. Her <u>nascent</u> medical skills allowed the resident to assist the elderly man when he collapsed in the subway.   C   I

4. Katrina was completely exhausted after <u>traversing</u> the north side of the city all day.   C   I

5. I had no choice; I was <u>entreated</u>.   C   I

6. Perhaps it is his training as an actor that allows George to become so <u>histrionic</u> when he is upset.   C   I

Matching

Instructions: Draw a line between words that have the same meaning.

oblivious	awe-inspiring
temporary break	forced
traversing	histrionics
not readily noticed	unmindful
entreated	gaudy
tenacious	conscious
sentient	inconspicuous
indigenous	traveling across
tastelessly showy	excessively controlling
nascent	native
elaborate public display	nomenclature
sublime	persistent
coerced	hiatus
a set of names	pageant
overly dramatic behavior	emerging
autocratic	requested urgently

Unit 9

New Words

Abstained	Iniquity
Audacious	Licentious
Infamy	

From inference to meaning

Instructions: Read the following excerpt from Cicero's "First Oration Against Lucus Catiline," in which the famous orator denounces Catiline, and use contextual information to guess the meanings of the underlined words. Then, have a look at the table below to see how accurately you guessed the meanings.

What sort of evilness is not stamped upon your life? What disgraceful circumstance is lacking from your <u>infamy</u> in private affairs? From what lustfulness have your eyes, from what atrocity have your hands, from what <u>iniquity</u> has your whole body ever <u>abstained</u>? Is there one youth, when you have once entangled him in the temptations of your corruption, to whom you have not held out a sword for <u>audacious</u> crime, or a torch for <u>licentious</u> wickedness?

Your Guesses

Abstained: _____   Iniquity: _____

Audacious: _____   Licentious: _____

Infamy: _____

Definitions

Abstained: willingly refrained from

Audacious: fearless; recklessly daring

Infamy: reputation for evil

Iniquity: wickedness

Licentious: sexually immoral; lacking in moral restraint

Word fuse

Instructions: Draw a line between each fragment in the left column and one fragment in the right column to create a word.

INI	ACIOUS
AB	QUITY
LICE	STAINED
AUD	FAMY
IN	NTIOUS

Fill-ins

Instructions: Fill in the blank in each sentence below with one of the words from the following list:

abstained   audacious   infamy   iniquity   licentious

1. The president of the school board has been accused of being _____, but he is in fact a devoted and faithful husband.

2. Briar's plan to hike the Italian Alps by herself next summer is quite _____!

3. After his conviction for allowing prisoners to be both verbally and physically abused, the warden's _____ quickly grew throughout the state.

4. Sid always _____ from alcohol on the night before an important exam.

5. The man's _____ was reflected in his extensive history of theft and assault.

Word scramble

Instructions: Unscramble each of the following words. Use the hints below as needed.

1) F I A Y M N _____

2) O C A A I S D U U _____

3) E S N I C U T I L O _____

4) Q U Y N T I I I _____

5) B A N D A E T S I _____

Hints:
1) reputation for evil, 2) fearless, 3) sexually immoral, 4) wickedness,
5) willingly refrained from

Matching

Instructions: Draw a line between words that have the same meaning.

wickedness   reputation for evil

infamy   sexually immoral

abstained   audacious

licentious   iniquity

fearless   willingly refrained from

Unit 10

New Words

Haphazardly   Throng
Humility   Unorthodox
Ingenuity   Variegated
Nonchalant   Winsome
Opulent   Wry

From inference to meaning

Instructions: Read the following passage and use contextual information to guess the meanings of the underlined words. Then, have a look at the table below to see how accurately you guessed the meanings.

At the arts festival I noticed an Asian man creating paintings using a most underlined unorthodox method. He had laid four canvases on the ground and was sprinkling colored powder onto each one haphazardly.

On a small table were small bowls of powder, each containing a different color; after emptying one bowl, he would go on to the next. He was a little man, in his seventies perhaps, with an innocent look in his eyes and a <u>winsome</u> smile. As he distributed the powder, his movements were quick and <u>nonchalant</u>, giving the impression that he was barely paying attention. Soon a <u>throng</u> of people had gathered to watch. He lifted each canvas upright and leaned it against his table. Then he took a large cloth and began fanning them. The excess powder fell away, leaving a large, <u>variegated</u> Chinese character on each canvas. The powders must have had something shiny in them, because each character reflected an <u>opulent</u> glitter in the morning light. The onlookers applauded. The man, who was clearly not arrogant about his work, nodded and smiled with an expression of <u>humility</u>. I approached him then to ask about his methods. He explained that he had begun by painting the character on each canvas in glue, and I praised him for his <u>ingenuity</u>. He made a <u>wry</u> face. "I'm trained as a calligrapher," he said. "This art I just do for money." He laughed, and I inquired about the price of the canvases.

Your Guesses

Haphazardly: _____   Throng: _____

Humility: _____   Unorthodox: _____

Ingenuity: _____   Variegated: _____

Nonchalant: _____   Winsome: _____

Opulent: _____   Wry: _____

Definitions

Haphazardly: carelessly; randomly

Humility: humbleness

Ingenuity: inventiveness; cleverness

Nonchalant: seemingly indifferent; cool and casual

Opulent: luxurious; rich

Throng: densely packed group; crowd

Unorthodox: unconventional

Variegated: multi-colored

Winsome: charming in a childlike way

Wry: sarcastic; momentarily twisted

Word fuse

Instructions: Draw a line between each fragment in the left column and one fragment in the right column to create a word.

VARI	SOME
HUM	HAZARDLY
NON	THODOX
W	CHALANT
HAP	NUITY
OP	EGATED
WIN	ONG
THR	ILITY
UNOR	RY
INGE	ULENT

Fill-ins

Instructions: Fill in the blank in each sentence below with one of the words from the following list:

haphazardly	humility	ingenuity	nonchalant	opulent
throng	unorthodox	variegated	winsome	wry

1. The student demonstrated his _____ by approaching the master quietly and addressing the old man in the most respectful language.

2. I don't want a plain old monochromatic suit; show me something bright and _____.

3. The day after George proposed, Liza showed up at work wearing the large and _____ ring he had given her.

4. My cousin's son is the most delightful, _____ little boy.

5. When I saw how _____ computer parts were strewn across Kayla's desk, I began to question whether I should allow her to fix my own computer.

6. J.T.'s habit of teasing customers during their initial contact with him is an _____ approach to selling cars.

7. With their deadline rapidly approaching, the other members of the research team found Myra's _____ attitude to be rather annoying.

8. With a _____ smile, Jake explained that he had been fired because he performed his job too well.

9. A _____ of people gathered at the scene of the accident.

10. Alma demonstrated great _____ by deriving the formula before anyone else in the class was even halfway finished.

■ Word scramble

Instructions: Unscramble each of the following words. Use the hints below as needed.

1) P E O T N L U _____

2) G D I A A E R E V T _____

3) Y N E U T N G I I _____

4) O O H X O T D R U N _____

5) I I U Y L M T H _____

6) Y W R _____

7) P Z Y H D A L A A H R _____

8) I S E N M W O _____

9) C N T O N A N L H A _____

10) N G H O T R _____

Hints:

1) luxurious, 2) multi-colored, 3) inventiveness, 4) unconventional, 5) humbleness,
6) sarcastic, 7) carelessly, 8) charming, 9) seemingly indifferent, 10) densely packed group

Matching

Instructions: Draw a line between words that have the same meaning.

wry	multi-colored
throng	opulent
unconventional	winsome
luxurious	humbleness
nonchalant	ingenuity
charming	densely packed group
humility	seemingly indifferent
variegated	sarcastic
inventiveness	unorthodox
opulent	luxurious

Review: Units 9 & 10

Contrasts

The adjectival form of "ingenuity" is "ingenious." Describing a person or a thing as ingenious is a reference to its cleverness. However, "ingenious" is easily confused with "ingenuous," which means "naive" or "innocent." For example:

He was such an *ingenious* man; by age 20 he had already invented several accounting software applications. However, because he was also *ingenuous*, he was unable to prevent other people from stealing his ideas.

Fast facts

1. The word "unorthodox" stems from the Greek words "un" (not), "ortho" ("right"), and "doxa" ("opinion"). An "unorthodox" belief is one that is not "right," in that it is unofficial or unconventional. One or more unorthodox beliefs can also be referred to as a "heterodoxy"—a belief or set of beliefs that differ from orthodox views.

2. The original meaning of the word "wry" is "contorted" or "twisted." (Often, a wry expression can be conveyed through a slight twisting of the mouth.) The same root can be seen in the word "awry," which means "crooked." For example:

Every now and then, the man adjusted the painting that hung over his fireplace; within a few days, the painting was slightly *awry* again. After several weeks, he realized that his efforts were futile. "What a powerful work of art," he muttered with a *wry* smile.

■ Grammar stretches

Instructions: Fill in the blank in each sentence below with one of the words from the following list. You may have to change the grammatical form of each word in order for it to fit into a sentence.

abstained	audacious	haphazardly	infamy	licentious
nonchalant	opulent	throng	wry	

1. I saw Martina for a moment before she disappeared into the crowd that was _____ into the stadium.

2. Although he had been a professional football player, Mr. Smith spoke _____ about that phase of his life and didn't seem to care whether or not other people knew of the details.

3. Given how many people in our society drink alcohol, it is impressive that you and your friends have chosen to _____.

4. The _____ nature of the Nazi regime is beyond dispute.

5. Because nobody knew what a difficult child Mr. Ingersoll's son had been, Ingersoll usually smiled _____ when he heard his son praised.

6. He was the first—and last—foot soldier to have had the _____ to request an audience with the king.

7. Gina was deeply impressed by the _____ of the Newport mansions, homes to some of the richest people in America many years ago.

8. Stan's choice of clothing today was rather _____, as he had only had five minutes to get ready in the morning.

9. After numerous affairs and other highly publicized sexual indiscretions, the actor's _____ had become common knowledge.

■ Error watch

Instructions: In the following sentences, note whether the underlined word is used correctly or not. Circle the C at the end of the sentence if the word is used correctly; circle the I if it is used incorrectly.

1. Lynn's four-year-old son has an <u>unorthodox</u> method of getting dressed, as he puts his shoes and socks on before his pants.   C   I

2. The man's <u>ingenuity</u> can be seen in his many criminal convictions and other instances of bad behavior.   C   I

3. Mere knowledge is insufficient; only someone with great <u>humility</u> could be resourceful enough to solve this particular design problem.   C   I

4. The way little Leanne screams when she gets frustrated is so <u>winsome</u>.   C   I

5. Before he was arrested, the killer's <u>iniquity</u> was the stuff of legend.   C   I

◼ Matching

Instructions: Draw a line between words that have the same meaning.

humbleness	wickedness
sarcastic	abstained
licentious	luxurious
willingly refrained from	haphazardly
variegated	ingenuity
densely packed group	wry
seemingly indifferent	reputation for evil
charming	throng
infamy	nonchalant
iniquity	sexually immoral
opulent	humility
carelessly	fearless
unorthodox	winsome
inventiveness	unconventional
audacious	multi-colored

Unit 11

New Words

Atrocious

Bulbous

Florid

Protruded

Surmounted

From inference to meaning

Instructions: Read the following excerpt from Flannery O'Connor's story "Everything that rises must converge," and use contextual information to guess the meanings of the underlined words. Then, have a look at the table below to see how accurately you guessed the meanings.

> She lifted the hat one more time and set it down slowly on top of her head. Two wings of gray hair <u>protruded</u> on either side of her <u>florid</u> face, but her eyes, sky-blue, were as innocent and untouched by experience as they must have been when she was ten. . . . He opened the door himself and started down the walk to get her going. The sky was a dying violet and the houses stood out darkly against it, <u>bulbous</u> liver-colored monstrosities of a uniform ugliness though no two were alike. Since this had been a fashionable neighborhood forty years ago, his mother persisted in thinking they did well to have an apartment in it. Each house had a narrow collar of dirt around it in which sat, usually, a grubby child. . . . The door closed and he turned to find the dumpy figure, <u>surmounted</u> by the <u>atrocious</u> hat, coming toward him.

Your Guesses

Atrocious: _____

Bulbous: _____

Florid: _____

Protruded: _____

Surmounted: _____

Definitions

Atrocious: exceptionally bad; brutal

Bulbous: swollen; rounded

Florid: reddish; excessively ornamented

Protruded: extended outward

Surmounted: topped; overcame

Word fuse

Instructions: Draw a line between each fragment in the left column and one fragment in the right column to create a word.

FLO	MOUNTED
PRO	TRUDED
BUL	RID
SUR	OCIOUS
ATR	BOUS

Fill-ins

Instructions: Fill in the blank in each sentence below with one of the words from the following list:

atrocious   bulbous   florid   protruded   surmounted

1. Paul's face was quite _____ after spending all day out in the sun.

2. The lizard's tail _____ from behind the rock.

3. In my opinion, her behavior was _____ and deserving of severe punishment.

4. Whereas most boxers have flattened noses after many years in the ring, Mike's nose was rather _____.

5. He had _____ many obstacles on his way to a successful career.

Word scramble

Instructions: Unscramble each of the following words. Use the hints below as needed.

1) L O S B B U U _____

2) D M U U T R O E N S _____

3) D O L R F I _____

4) O T I S U C R O A _____

5) E U T R D D R P O _____

Hints:
1) swollen, 2) topped, 3) reddish, 4) exceptionally bad, 5) extended outward

▌ Matching

Instructions: Draw a line between words that have the same meaning.

reddish   topped

protruded   atrocious

bulbous   swollen

exceptionally bad   extended outward

surmounted   florid

▌ Unit 12

New Words

Hortatory	Nepotism
Inaugural	Opined
Inculcate	Weal
Munificent	Zealot

▌ From inference to meaning

Instructions: Read the following passage and use contextual information to guess the meanings of the underlined words. Then, have a look at the table below to see how accurately you guessed the meanings.

Today our mayor made a <u>hortatory</u> speech at a town hall meeting in order to encourage citizens to support her latest project, the development of a bid to host the Olympic Games. Not surprisingly, the theme of her speech was that hosting the Olympics would greatly benefit to the public <u>weal</u>. The mayor reassured citizens that funding for the venture would be provided by several of the most <u>munificent</u> local businesses rather than through tax dollars. She promised that there would be no <u>nepotism</u> in the awarding of contracts to build an Olympic stadium. And then, being a bit of a <u>zealot</u> about amateur athletics, she told a long story about attending the 1984 Summer Olympics herself while still a high school student in Los Angeles. An avid runner, she described how the 1984 games were host to the <u>inaugural</u> marathon for women. It was an inspiring moment for female athletes. She <u>opined</u> that just as she had been inspired by those female marathoners to strive for excellence in her own career, so the presence of the Olympic games in our city would help <u>inculcate</u> an appreciation for success among a new generation of students as they come of age.

Your Guesses

Hortatory: _____   Nepotism: _____

Inaugural: _____   Opined: _____

Inculcate: _____   Weal: _____

Munificent: _____   Zealot: _____

Definitions

Hortatory: strongly encouraging

Inaugural: initial; formally marking a beginning

Inculcate: instill; indoctrinate

Munificent: extremely generous

Nepotism: favoritism toward family or friends by someone in power

Opined: expressed opinion

Weal: prosperity; well-being

Zealot: fanatic

■ Word fuse

Instructions: Draw a line between each fragment in the left column and one fragment in the right column to create a word.

MUN	OT
OPI	AL
ZEAL	IFICENT
NE	TATORY
INA	POTISM
WE	NED
IN	UGURAL
HOR	CULCATE

■ Fill-ins

Instructions: Fill in the blank in each sentence below with one of the words from the following list:

hortatory	inaugural	inculcate	munificent	nepotism
opined	weal	zealot		

1. In teaching his students carpentry, Steve tries to _____ in them respect for the materials and an appreciation of the craft.

2. My interest is not in protecting the wealthiest citizens, since they can take care of themselves, but rather in promoting the common _____.

3. Even when his team was winning by a large margin, Coach Brown's halftime speeches were always strongly _____.

4. Gifts from its most _____ citizens have allowed the town to remodel city hall.

5. Alice is a _____ about promoting clean energy whenever she can.

6. He planned to attend the _____ ceremony marking the opening of his best friend's charter school.

7. "We need a new governor," _____ Timothy, "and we need one now."

8. As his uncle is vice president of our company, it seems he got his job through _____ rather than his own qualifications.

■ Word scramble

Instructions: Unscramble each of the following words. Use the hints below as needed.

1) T N I E L U C C A _____

2) E N P O I D _____

3) T Y T O O A H R R _____

4) R A L U N A G I U _____

5) A E O L Z T _____

6) M I S T O N P E _____

7) L A W E _____

8) C I U T M I N N F E _____

Hints:
1) instill, 2) expressed opinion, 3) strongly encouraging, 4) initial, 5) fanatic, 6) favoritism, 7) prosperity, 8) extremely generous

Matching

Instructions: Draw a line between words that have the same meaning.

prosperity   instill

nepotism   munificent

hortatory   expressed opinion

extremely generous   inaugural

zealot   fanatic

initial   weal

opined   strongly encouraging

inculcate   favoritism

Review: Units 11 & 12

Contrasts

It is easy to confuse vocabulary words that differ by only one or two sounds. For example: "Weal" refers to prosperity, while "zeal" refers to enthusiasm. "Munificent" refers to generosity, while "magnificent" refers to grandeur. However, "hortatory" and "exhortatory" have approximately the same meaning.

Fast facts

1. The adjective "munificent" comes from the Latin word "munus," which means "gift" or "service." "Munus" appears in other English words as well, such as "remunerate" (i.e., repay) and "immune" (i.e., exempt or free). For example:

   During the election, the mayor realized that some people might be critical of how much he spent on *remunerating* industry leaders for speaking at campaign events, but he paid them in full anyway because he was largely *immune* to criticism.

2. Words develop different meanings over time, but newer meanings do not always replace older ones. For example:

   (a) In reference to a person's face, "florid" refers to a flushed or reddish color. In reference to a person's speech or writing, "florid" means flowery, or excessively ornamented.

   (b) In reference to objects, "surmounted" indicates that one object was on top of another one. Used abstractly, "surmounted" means that someone or something overcame a challenge.

   (c) In reference to groups or individuals, "weal" refers to prosperity or well-being. As a physical description, a "weal" is a raised mark on the skin resulting from injury or allergy.

■ Grammar stretches

Instructions: Fill in the blank in each sentence below with one of the words from the following list. You may have to change the grammatical form of each word in order for it to fit into a sentence.

atrocious	florid	inaugural	munificent	nepotism
opined	protruded	surmounted	zealot	

1. My daughter is not very good yet at playing hide-and-seek; whenever she hides behind something, some part of her is always _____.

2. The executive quite _____ awarded the summer internship to his niece.

3. The number of _____ committed by their militia against ordinary citizens will never be fully revealed.

4. Although she had received an invitation, Patty was unable to attend the _____ of the new governor.

5. If you try hard enough, you can _____ any obstacle.

6. Noriko is so _____ about cleanliness; she actually cleans her apartment two or three times a week!

7. The anonymous donor's _____ allowed the city to build a new park in the downtown area.

8. Because I don't know the facts of the Wilson case, I am unable to share with you my _____ as to his innocence.

9. The teacher did not appreciate the _____ of Jenn's wordy style.

■ Error watch

Instructions: In the following sentences, note whether the underlined word is used correctly or not. Circle the C at the end of the sentence if the word is used correctly; circle the I if it is used incorrectly.

1. Jon listened to the complaint with a <u>weal</u> expression on his face.   C   I

2. I had thought that my mother's speech to me about the importance of finishing college would be threatening; instead, what she said turned out to be enthusiastic and <u>hortatory</u>.   C   I

3. His forehead was not merely large; it was downright <u>bulbous</u>.   C   I

4. Today is the one-month anniversary of Mykala's <u>inculcation</u> as president of our organization.   C   I

5. The criminal's gun <u>surmounted</u> from his coat pocket.   C   I

■ Matching

Instructions: Draw a line between words that have the same meaning.

extended outward	opined
hortatory	zealot
extremely generous	reddish
fanatic	munificent
inculcate	topped
nepotism	instill
bulbous	initial
florid	favoritism
exceptionally bad	protruded
inaugural	swollen
prosperity	strongly encouraging
expressed opinion	weal
surmounted	atrocious

■ Word Search

Instructions: All of the new words from Units 11 and 12 are hidden in this challenging puzzle. The words may be written forwards or backwards in any direction: horizontal, vertical, or diagonal. Some words overlap in one letter. Your task is to circle each word once you have found it.

Following are the meanings of the words you're looking for. (Remember: You're searching for the actual words, not the meanings given here.)

swollen	topped	reddish	exceptionally bad
extended outward	instill	strongly encouraging	
expressed opinion	fanatic	prosperity	
favoritism	initial		
extremely generous			

```
B  I  T  O  L  A  E  Z  O  O  P  N  I  C  E  E  G  R  A  S
M  U  L  L  E  R  L  E  S  P  R  O  T  R  U  D  E  D  U  S
E  A  L  E  S  T  B  A  C  T  U  S  C  I  C  T  I  D  L  H
N  G  I  B  H  M  P  K  E  F  V  T  A  H  V  F  N  T  S  A
C  R  R  F  O  Q  R  T  I  R  A  X  T  B  S  E  N  N  T  I
H  E  O  E  J  U  K  E  Z  R  P  T  T  P  O  E  K  E  W  R
O  A  L  W  S  A  S  P  E  O  Y  Y  R  C  P  Y  O  C  S  D
R  I  G  D  O  T  R  U  T  L  S  O  F  O  D  Q  N  I  A  A
T  O  I  E  F  L  O  R  I  D  U  B  T  E  C  U  A  F  H  N
A  S  O  N  E  T  A  N  N  D  N  I  T  N  A  I  T  I  U  J
T  A  V  I  C  H  A  Z  T  E  S  A  L  E  R  F  O  N  T  E
O  R  Y  T  F  U  N  O  I  M  T  N  E  R  M  E  B  U  O  D
R  T  E  W  G  O  L  O  W  P  R  O  F  B  A  W  L  M  S  G
Y  E  L  U  K  T  I  C  D  E  N  I  P  O  L  G  Y  O  P  A
N  U  R  Z  O  D  T  R  A  T  O  X  S  A  L  O  A  B  H  L
E  A  T  L  B  X  H  A  I  T  Y  E  I  R  O  V  I  N  U  P
L  R  Y  E  C  T  H  N  C  R  E  V  T  E  C  A  W  E  N  E
S  A  L  E  D  E  T  N  U  O  M  R  U  S  L  S  U  P  L  E
C  R  I  G  A  D  E  R  P  P  O  L  E  R  R  O  W  E  A  L
```

ANSWER KEY: CHAPTER 2

Unit 1

Word fuse

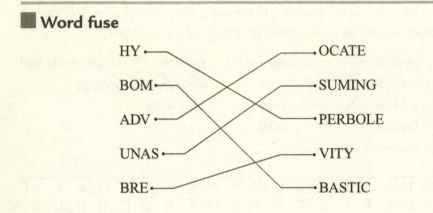

Fill-ins

1. **_Brevity_** is called for in this situation, because we are running short of time.

2. Jerome wanted to become a congressman so that he could **_advocate_** for the people's interests.

3. Once you have achieved great success, the more **_unassuming_** you are in your dealings with people, the more they will respect you.

4. I admit that my car isn't beautiful, but to call it the ugliest and most useless piece of machinery you've ever seen is just plain **_hyperbole_**.

5. During the discussion, Beverly had become so **_bombastic_** that even those who supported her point of view grew weary of her speeches.

■ Word scramble

1) UNASSUMING

2) BREVITY

3) HYPERBOLE

4) BOMBASTIC

5) ADVOCATE

■ Matching

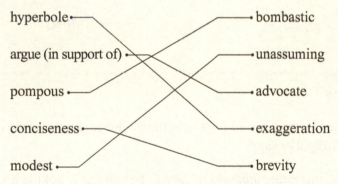

hyperbole → bombastic

argue (in support of) → unassuming

pompous → advocate

conciseness → exaggeration

modest → brevity

Unit 2

Word fuse

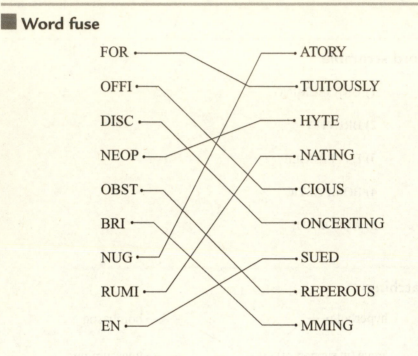

FOR •   • ATORY

OFFI •   • TUITOUSLY

DISC •   • HYTE

NEOP •   • NATING

OBST •   • CIOUS

BRI •   • ONCERTING

NUG •   • SUED

RUMI •   • REPEROUS

EN •   • MMING

Fill-ins

1. The two men argued for a long time before one shoved the other and a fistfight _**ensued**_.

2. It seems rather _**officious**_ of Jack to be constantly poking his nose into Adrianna's business and telling her what to do.

3. From his _**morose**_ expression I could tell that he was depressed.

4. Sometimes I am envious of the way children wake up every morning _**brimming**_ with energy.

5. You will never catch Tricia _**ruminating**_ about how to handle a difficult situation; rather, she acts decisively and never second-guesses herself.

6. It is not easy to negotiate a compromise with an _**obstreperous**_ person.

7. The teacher found it somewhat _**disconcerting**_ that his best student did so poorly on the most recent test.

8. Because nobody enforces this particular regulation, industry leaders consider it _**nugatory**_.

9. While driving across town, the engine of Brittany's car suddenly cut off; _**fortuitously**_, she rolled to a stop less than 50 yards from a garage.

10. He plays guitar quite well for a _**neophyte**_.

■ Word scramble

1) DISCONCERTING

2) OBSTREPEROUS

3) MOROSE

4) ENSUED

5) NUGATORY

6) RUMINATING

7) BRIMMING

8) OFFICIOUS

9) NEOPHYTE

10) FORTUITOUS

■ Matching

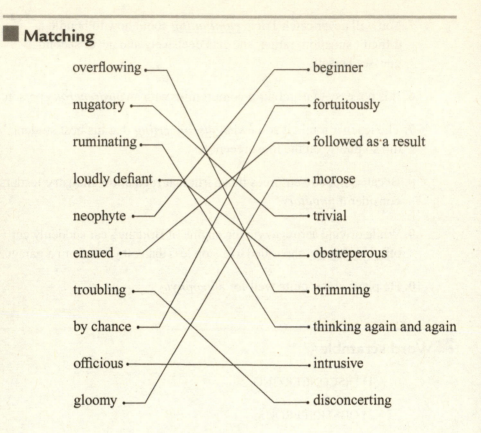

overflowing   beginner

nugatory   fortuitously

ruminating   followed as a result

loudly defiant   morose

neophyte   trivial

ensued   obstreperous

troubling   brimming

by chance   thinking again and again

officious   intrusive

gloomy   disconcerting

Review: Units 1 & 2

Grammar stretches

1. After waiting in line for several hours, the fans rushed into the stadium when the gates opened, and many people got shoved around or stepped on in the ***ensuing*** chaos.

2. "Since I got laid off," Martin whispered ***morosely***, "I've been feeling too unhappy to look for another job."

3. How ***fortuitous*** that Professor Jones canceled class on the very day I was too sick to attend!

4. The poorest citizens of their country lack political power because no one has ***advocated*** effectively for their interests.

5. Following the interview, Ariel ***ruminated*** for several hours about her performance, imagining the various answers she could have made to the interviewer's questions.

6. Whenever Brad's Aunt visited him, she would snoop around his apartment, ask him personal questions, offer detailed advice on virtually every topic, and otherwise aggravate him with her ***officiousness***.

7. It ***disconcerted*** me to look into the mirror each morning and see the gray hairs gradually crowding out the darker ones.

8. Riley was a shy child who spoke quietly and ***unassumingly***, and rarely caused her teachers any trouble.

9. The ***neophytes*** in our group need to be a little more respectful of the old-timers, in my opinion.

10. As Mr. Matthews grew more ill, his natural ***obstreperousness*** increased, and he became less and less willing to cooperate with the nurses.

11. He spoke of his younger daughter in a voice that ***brimmed*** with affection and pride.

◼ Error watch

1. If you continue to speak with such <u>brevity</u>, your audience will lose interest; keep your speeches short!   **Incorrect**

2. Joe claims that on this particular stretch of road the speed limit is <u>nugatory</u>, because it's never enforced by the police.   **Correct**

3. The congressman has an undistinguished record thus far; it seems like cheap <u>hyperbole</u> to compare him to Abraham Lincoln.   **Correct**

4. Following the accident, the two drivers stood toe-to-toe, shouting at each other <u>fortuitously</u>.   **Incorrect**

5. He shook his head <u>bombastically</u>, saddened by the comment his uncle had just made.   **Incorrect**

6. Jolene was quite <u>disconcerted</u> to discover a leak in her roof.   **Correct**

Matching

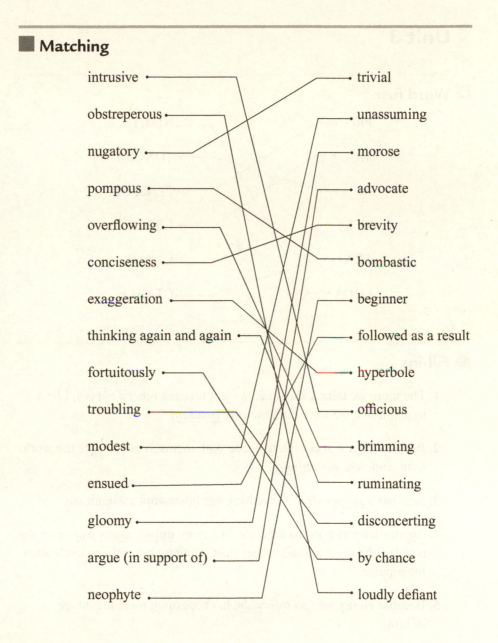

intrusive	trivial
obstreperous	unassuming
nugatory	morose
pompous	advocate
overflowing	brevity
conciseness	bombastic
exaggeration	beginner
thinking again and again	followed as a result
fortuitously	hyperbole
troubling	officious
modest	brimming
ensued	ruminating
gloomy	disconcerting
argue (in support of)	by chance
neophyte	loudly defiant

Unit 3

Word fuse

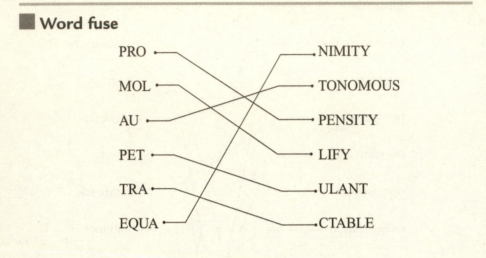

Fill-ins

1. The more we talked, the more we got on each other's nerves; I have to admit that we were both awfully ***petulant***.

2. People who are at complete peace with themselves can face the world with complete ***equanimity***.

3. Jada has a ***propensity*** to overthink her homework assignments.

4. Agency leaders hope to function in a more ***autonomous*** way once the new legislation is passed, rather than continuing to rely on each other for support.

5. Because Henry was so ***tractable***, his boss often took advantage of him.

6. No matter how hard I tried, I was unable to ***mollify*** the angry woman.

Word scramble

1) PROPENSITY

2) AUTONOMOUS

3) MOLLIFY

4) TRACTABLE

5) EQUANIMITY

6) PETULANT

Matching

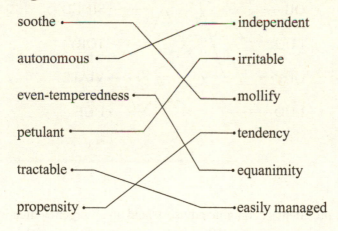

Unit 4

Word fuse

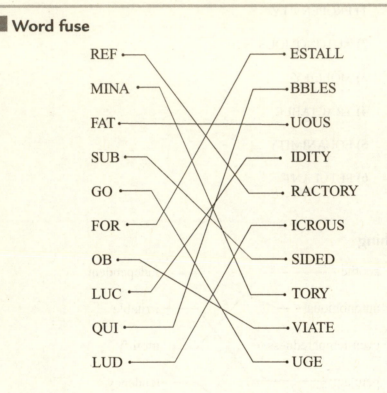

REF — ESTALL
MINA — BBLES
FAT — UOUS
SUB — IDITY
GO — RACTORY
FOR — ICROUS
OB — SIDED
LUC — TORY
QUI — VIATE
LUD — UGE

Fill-ins

1. The president's economic advisors held an emergency meeting to discuss how to _**forestall**_ the country's imminent financial crisis.

2. Like a _**refractory**_ child, the patient refused to take his medicine.

3. Lonnie has never stolen anything in his entire life; the allegation that he took Rosalind's purse is completely _**ludicrous**_.

4. With a _**fatuous**_ smile, the student walked up to the blackboard and proceeded to write down the wrong answer to the teacher's question.

5. As the committee worked together on a draft of the document, there were numerous _**quibbles**_ about minor details of the wording.

6. Because of his great size, a scowling expression, and the prominent scar on one cheek, John had a rather _**minatory**_ appearance.

7. Once the floodwaters had _**subsided**_, the engineers were able to evaluate the extent of the damage.

8. Wearing a helmet while riding a bicycle can _**obviate**_ the risk of injury.

9. Watkins' argument before the high court was remarkable for both its passion as well as its _**lucidity**_.

10. This particular corporation has a nasty tendency to _**gouge**_ its clients at every opportunity.

■ Word scramble

      1) LUCIDITY

      2) QUIBBLES

      3) OBVIATE

      4) FORESTALL

      5) REFRACTORY

      6) LUDICROUS

      7) MINATORY

      8) GOUGE

      9) FATUOUS

     10) SUBSIDED

■ Matching

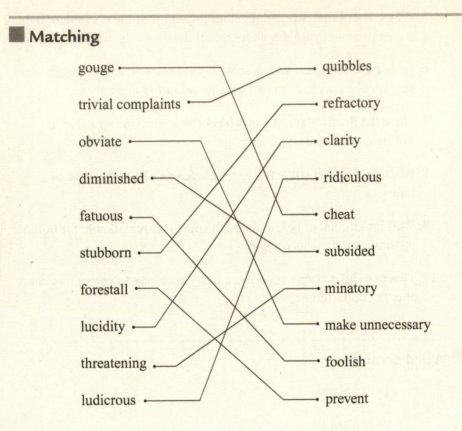

gouge	quibbles
trivial complaints	refractory
obviate	clarity
diminished	ridiculous
fatuous	cheat
stubborn	subsided
forestall	minatory
lucidity	make unnecessary
threatening	foolish
ludicrous	prevent

Review: Units 3 & 4

Fill-ins

1. Our pricing structure varies from project to project, but our company would never *gouge* a client.

2. The invading army was a dark and *minatory* presence in the daily lives of the villagers.

3. Matthias was a great leader because he handled all situations, whether urgent, frightening, or complex, with the same *equanimity* and poise.

4. I believe that the conflict in our schedules is *tractable* and thus easily remedied.

5. My father was raised in a conservative household, and so he considers tattoos, piercings, and other forms of body art to be *ludicrous*.

6. Being such a generous woman, Martha had a *propensity* to donate to every charitable organization that approached her.

Grammar stretches

1. Once Robbie loses his temper, very little can be done by way of *mollifying* him.

2. Given the extent of her *refractoriness*, it is no surprise that their foreign minister refused to renegotiate our original trade agreement.

3. The social studies teacher was impressed by how clearly organized and *lucid* Tim's paper turned out to be.

4. Liz was capable of exceptional *petulance*, pouting and complaining whenever someone disagreed with her or failed to do things her way.

5. Although his wife was gravely ill, Gerald continued to be preoccupied with improving his golf game, reducing his waistline, and otherwise behaving *fatuously*.

6. Our disagreement about the third item of the contract is merely a *quibble* rather than representing a fundamental difference.

7. Instead of consulting with the manager every time you make a personnel-related decision, we would like you to handle your decision-making more *autonomously*.

8. Prior to describing the new semiconductor technology, the engineering professor made some comments to the class that *forestalled* any confusion about what would be covered on the next test.

9. Not until her anger *subsides* will Francine be able to approach her brother about his indiscretions.

10. He used to think that brushing and flossing one's teeth regularly *obviates* the need for regular visits to the dentist.

■ Error watch

1. I wish my younger son were more cooperative instead of being so minatory about every little detail and doing things his own way.   **Incorrect**

2. Sheila met every crisis with admirable equanimity and poise.   **Correct**

3. By treating the wound yourself, you will mollify the need for a doctor.   **Incorrect**

4. It is obviate that Rita loves algebra.   **Incorrect**

5. Farley is not a refractory person, even though he has strong opinions and is quite capable of standing up for them.   **Correct**

■ Matching

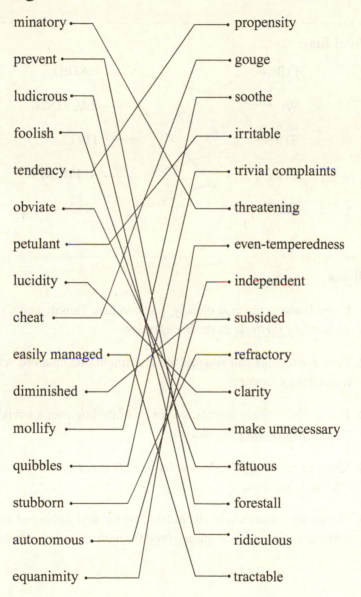

minatory	propensity
prevent	gouge
ludicrous	soothe
foolish	irritable
tendency	trivial complaints
obviate	threatening
petulant	even-temperedness
lucidity	independent
cheat	subsided
easily managed	refractory
diminished	clarity
mollify	make unnecessary
quibbles	fatuous
stubborn	forestall
autonomous	ridiculous
equanimity	tractable

Unit 5

Word fuse

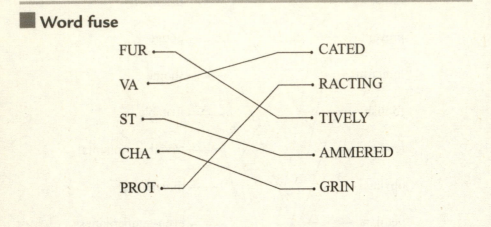

Fill-ins

1. If you listen to the tape closely, you can hear Tammy and Cyndi whispering _**furtively**_ in the background.

2. Once the tenants had _**vacated**_ the apartment, the landlord was able to replace the carpeting.

3. The two committee members kept on quibbling over a trivial point, thereby _**protracting**_ the meeting.

4. Much to her _**chagrin**_, Melissa realized that her comment had deeply offended their host.

5. The witness was clearly intimidated by the atmosphere of the courtroom and consequently _**stammered**_ through most of his testimony.

Word scramble

1) STAMMERED

2) CHAGRIN

3) VACATED

4) PROTRACTING

5) FURTIVELY

Matching

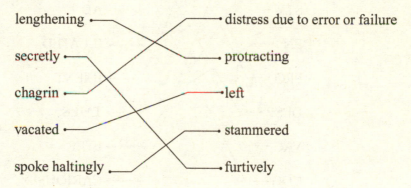

lengthening — distress due to error or failure

secretly — protracting

chagrin — left

vacated — stammered

spoke haltingly — furtively

Unit 6

Word fuse

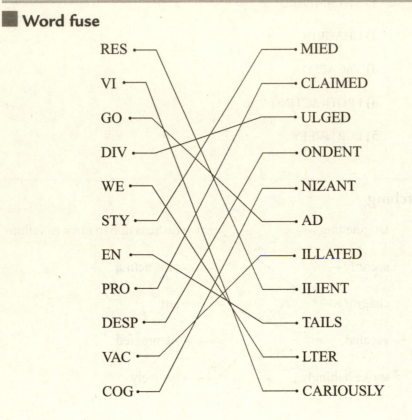

RES   MIED

VI   CLAIMED

GO   ULGED

DIV   ONDENT

WE   NIZANT

STY   AD

EN   ILLATED

PRO   ILIENT

DESP   TAILS

VAC   LTER

COG   CARIOUSLY

■ Fill-ins

1. They *vacillated* too long and the opportunity was lost.

2. After failing three classes last semester, Blake became *despondent* and decided to drop out of college.

3. Today the leaders of the two countries *proclaimed* that a new era of peace between them had arrived.

4. If you continue to *goad* Darla with complaints about her attitude, she is likely to respond by becoming even less cooperative.

5. Phil was deeply involved in every aspect of his son's life, and his mood was closely linked to his son's successes and failures; many people thought that Phil was living *vicariously* through the boy.

6. The neurosurgeon began the delicate process of removing the tumor, fully *cognizant* of the fact that that the slightest mistake could cause further damage.

7. Abe's desk was a *welter* of books, articles, and papers, along with photographs of his three children, an ashtray or two, and the occasional soda can.

8. Because she is so *resilient*, I'm sure Debbie will overcome this latest setback.

9. Jim's wife wanted to know exactly how much information he had *divulged* to friends about their last quarrel.

10. Efforts by the two senators to gather support for their tax reform bill were *stymied* by a lack of public support for the bill.

11. Being the accountant for this particular company *entails* more than the usual range of responsibilities.

■ Word scramble

1) DIVULGE

2) STYMIED

3) WELTER

4) COGNIZANT

5) RESILIENT

6) VICARIOUSLY

7) GOAD

8) DESPONDENT

9) PROCLAIMED

10) VACILLATED

11) ENTAILS

■ Matching

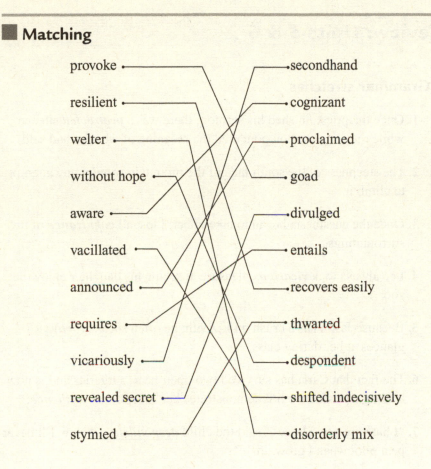

provoke	secondhand
resilient	cognizant
welter	proclaimed
without hope	goad
aware	divulged
vacillated	entails
announced	recovers easily
requires	thwarted
vicariously	despondent
revealed secret	shifted indecisively
stymied	disorderly mix

Review: Units 5 & 6

■ Grammar stretches

1. Once the priest finished his sermon, there was a ***protracted*** silence while the congregation pondered the meaning of what he had said.

2. The steepness of the south face of the mountain ***stymies*** any attempt to climb it.

3. Once the anesthesia began to take effect, I lost all ***cognizance*** of my surroundings.

4. Lee always took ***vicarious*** pleasure at seeing his daughter enjoy the zoo.

5. Because Jason has a crush on Lizbeth, he often sneaks ***furtive*** glances at her during class.

6. The fact that Carla has survived two open-heart surgeries and is now leading a productive life demonstrates her exceptional ***resilience***.

7. "I hate my new glasses," said the child ***despondently***. "Now I'll never be a pilot when I grow up."

8. Kylie's boss is so intimidating that most of her colleagues end up ***stammering*** whenever they speak to him.

9. My best friend and I were both ***vacillating*** about whether to go to Miami or to Key West for spring break.

10. After being ***goaded*** by his wife for years to get into shape, Louis finally joined a local gym and began working out.

11. The staff sergeant was arrested for ***divulging*** military secrets to non-military personnel.

12. The eviction notice stated that the man must *vacate* the building immediately.

13. In the movie, the hero stands on a car to loudly *proclaim* his love for his girlfriend.

14. Asking my mother for money used to *entail* hearing a speech from her about the importance of financial planning.

Error watch

1. Leena could barely walk into her room due to the *welter* of clothes, books, and guitars that seemed to fill every available space.   Correct

2. My sister is so *vicarious*; she has the hardest time making up her mind.   Incorrect

3. The realization that she had spent almost a decade attempting to salvage a marriage that was ultimately doomed filled her with *chagrin*.   Correct

4. The organization's plans to register new voters were repeatedly *divulged* by logistical challenges.   Incorrect

5. After a *protracted* illness, Nima's poodle finally recovered.   Correct

6. I am not *cognizant* of any objection to the advice of this committee.   Correct

■ Matching

lengthening   secretly

entails   goad

provoke   vicariously

recovers easily   left

vacated   vacillated

secondhand   protracting

despondent   resilient

furtively   proclaim

distress due to   chagrin
error or failure

welter   stymied

shifted indecisively   spoke haltingly

cognizant   disorderly mix

revealed (a secret)   divulged

thwarted   aware

announce   without hope

stammered   requires

Word Search

```
C P E R M S H O E F D E M I A L C O R P
O R A D E S P O N D E N T S L O W L O O
G A S O L S C R A I P O W H I R E A S L
N T L D E O I I M S D E I M Y T S A V E
I A X O E R S L Y U N X L Y W O T U M E
Z E A B R K E V I N O G L J E D E V H N
A V N L U N Y I M E M N I E V E A E I R
N A W M T O P I R F N I S U A B N P W R
T C L A R A L D E O S T A M M E R E D O
M I I T E L I N G S D C H N E E L A J E
E L L F N V H O R T E A M E I T E E N N
S L T Q U A R A L G R R O R E L G O A D
I A U L N R E V O M I T A R M E A D L E
E T G S E P T I S D M O L U A S C L O T
T E E D S Z Y I M O P R Q U S R T U Y A
D D A R A O M T V R S P O N I R G A H C
R O B E W K A N C E Y G U G K E A L A A
E T S U E T H S T E L L V U A I W L I V
M V I C A R I O U S L Y E K N A G E L O
```

Unit 7

Word fuse

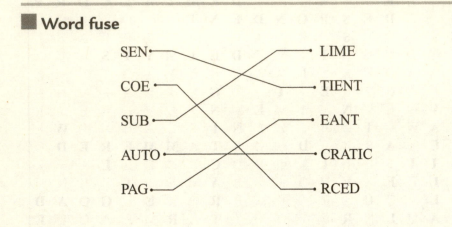

Fill-ins

1. The third graders at Kelley's school put on a delightful ***pageant*** to celebrate the arrival of spring.

2. Our trip to southern Italy last summer was absolutely ***sublime***.

3. Did the soldiers volunteer for this assignment, or were they ***coerced*** by their commanding officer?

4. Bill was an avid astronomer and science fiction buff who hoped that someday ***sentient*** beings would be discovered on some distant planet.

5. Even at home, the executive exhibited a disturbingly ***autocratic*** personality; at all times he expected compliance from his wife and obedience from his children.

Word scramble

1) SUBLIME

2) SENTIENT

3) AUTOCRATIC

4) PAGEANT

5) COERCED

Matching

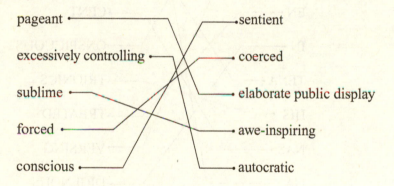

pageant

excessively controlling

sublime

forced

conscious

sentient

coerced

elaborate public display

awe-inspiring

autocratic

Unit 8

Word fuse

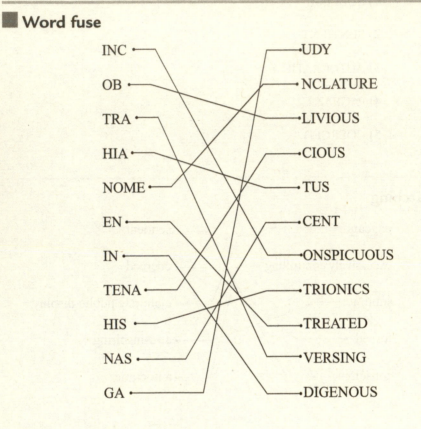

INC	UDY
OB	NCLATURE
TRA	LIVIOUS
HIA	CIOUS
NOME	TUS
EN	CENT
IN	ONSPICUOUS
TENA	TRIONICS
HIS	TREATED
NAS	VERSING
GA	DIGENOUS

Fill-ins

1. Jean is taking a little *hiatus* from work this week in order to attend to some personal matters.

2. It amazes me sometimes how *oblivious* my young son can be to the fact that one of his shoelaces is untied, or that he has peanut butter smeared on his pants, or that he has put his shirt on backwards.

3. Having learned the ***nomenclature*** for describing the various types of beer, Ralph enjoyed showing off his newfound knowledge to his friends.

4. An experienced spy knows how to be present and yet ***inconspicuous***.

5. Carly's diamond-encrusted pendant is one of the largest and most ***gaudy*** pieces of jewelry I have seen in years.

6. If you are sufficiently ***tenacious***, you can achieve almost anything.

7. The Yanomamo are an ***indigenous*** people who live in the upper Amazon region of South America.

8. Last year Marquis started his own consulting firm; he worked long hours at first as he sought to attract clients to his ***nascent*** business.

9. Although as a child he had been bitten by a rattlesnake there, Dan's fondness for ***traversing*** the Arizona desert was as strong as it had ever been.

10. A hint of desperation crept into her voice as Janet ***entreated*** the ticket agent to sell her a seat on the next flight.

11. I wasn't impressed by the actor's ***histrionics***; I felt that he exaggerated his character's inner torment to the point of caricature.

Word scramble

1) TENACIOUS

2) INCONSPICUOUS

3) HISTRIONICS

4) NASCENT

5) ENTREATED

6) NOMENCLATURE

7) HIATUS

8) TRAVERSING

9) OBLIVIOUS

10) GAUDY

11) INDIGENOUS

■ Matching

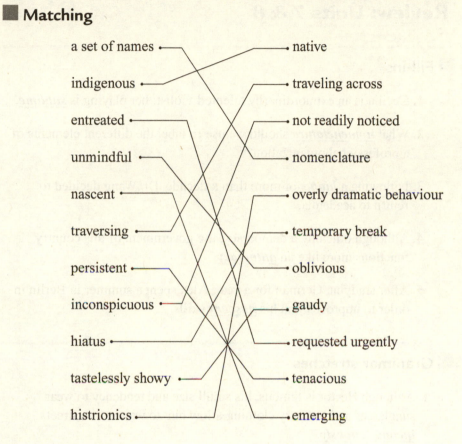

a set of names — native

indigenous — traveling across

entreated — not readily noticed

unmindful — nomenclature

nascent — overly dramatic behaviour

traversing — temporary break

persistent — oblivious

inconspicuous — gaudy

hiatus — requested urgently

tastelessly showy — tenacious

histrionics — emerging

Review: Units 7 & 8

▪ Fill-ins

1. Cecilia is an extraordinarily talented violist; her playing is **_sublime_**.

2. What **_nomenclature_** should we use to label the different elements of a professional organization?

3. Following a **_hiatus_** of more than a decade, Dr. Wang decided to return to academia.

4. Although officially a democracy, the government of this country functions more like an **_autocracy_**.

5. After studying German for a year, Alex spent a summer in Berlin in order to improve upon his **_nascent_** skills.

▪ Grammar stretches

1. Although Hector is famous, his small size and tendency to wear sunglasses and ordinary clothing allow him to wander the streets **_inconspicuously_**.

2. The police officer was found guilty of **_coercing_** the suspect to sign a confession.

3. Some people believe that only human beings are capable of **_sentience_**; however, I think it's clear that animals are conscious, and that they have the capacity to reflect on themselves and their surroundings.

4. Both cars are extraordinary, but the bright purple Cadillac with gold trim is definitely the **_gaudier_** of the two.

5. Someday Lillian hopes to **_traverse_** the Australian outback with her older brothers.

6. The more Peter ignored her, the more *histrionically* Patricia registered her dissatisfaction, with heavy sighs, pointed looks, and melodramatic remarks.

7. The child dug into his ice cream with such *tenacity* that within seconds the bowl was empty.

8. Such *obliviousness*! How could you forget the two things I asked you to buy at the grocery store?

9. The giant panda is *indigenous* to western China.

10. Carmen believed that if she kept on *entreating* her boss to let her take an extra week off in June, her boss would eventually agree to the plan.

11. Denzel loves the *pageantry* of the New Year's Day parade in our city.

◼ Error watch

1. Good thing Mike was so *oblivious*; otherwise he would have never convinced his teacher to give him an extension on the term paper.
Incorrect

2. It would be better for you to remain *indigenous* rather than allowing the two men to see you.   Incorrect

3. Her *nascent* medical skills allowed the resident to assist the elderly man when he collapsed in the subway.   Correct

4. Katrina was completely exhausted after *traversing* the north side of the city all day.   Correct

5. I had no choice; I was *entreated*.   Incorrect

6. Perhaps it is his training as an actor that allows George to become so *histrionic* when he is upset.   Correct

■ Matching

oblivious	awe-inspiring
temporary break	forced
traversing	histrionics
not readily noticed	unmindful
entreated	gaudy
tenacious	conscious
sentient	inconspicuous
indigenous	traveling across
tastelessly showy	excessively controlling
nascent	native
elaborate public display	nomenclature
sublime	persistent
coerced	hiatus
a set of names	pageant
overly dramatic behavior	emerging
autocratic	requested urgently

Unit 9

Word fuse

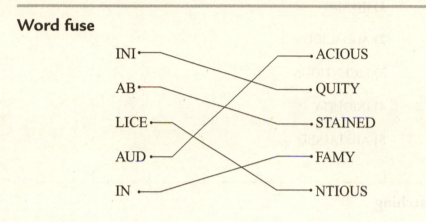

INI	ACIOUS
AB	QUITY
LICE	STAINED
AUD	FAMY
IN	NTIOUS

Fill-ins

1. The president of the school board has been accused of being *licentious*, but he is in fact a devoted and faithful husband.

2. Briar's plan to hike the Italian Alps by herself next summer is quite *audacious*!

3. After his conviction for allowing prisoners to be both verbally and physically abused, the warden's *infamy* quickly grew throughout the state.

4. Sid always *abstained* from alcohol on the night before an important exam.

5. The man's *iniquity* was reflected in his extensive history of theft and assault.

Word scramble

1) INFAMY

2) AUDACIOUS

3) LICENTIOUS

4) INIQUITY

5) ABSTAINED

Matching

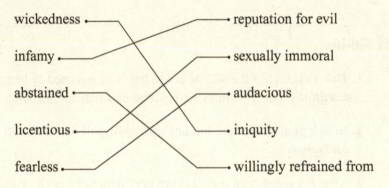

Unit 10

Word fuse

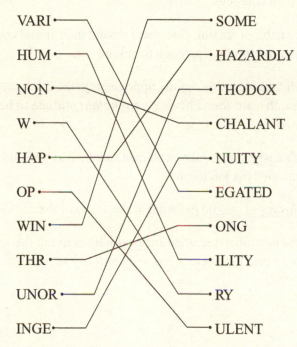

VARI
HUM
NON
W
HAP
OP
WIN
THR
UNOR
INGE

SOME
HAZARDLY
THODOX
CHALANT
NUITY
EGATED
ONG
ILITY
RY
ULENT

Fill-ins

1. The student demonstrated his *humility* by approaching the master quietly and addressing the old man in the most respectful language.

2. I don't want a plain old monochromatic suit; show me something bright and *variegated*.

3. The day after George proposed, Liza showed up at work wearing the large and *opulent* ring he had given her.

4. My cousin's son is the most delightful, **_winsome_** little boy.

5. When I saw how **_haphazardly_** computer parts were strewn across Kayla's desk, I began to question whether I should allow her to fix my own computer.

6. J.T.'s habit of teasing customers during their initial contact with him is an **_unorthodox_** approach to selling cars.

7. With their deadline rapidly approaching, the other members of the research team found Myra's **_nonchalant_** attitude to be rather annoying.

8. With a **_wry_** smile, Jake explained that he had been fired because he performed his job too well.

9. A **_throng_** of people gathered at the scene of the accident.

10. Alma demonstrated great **_ingenuity_** by deriving the formula before anyone else in the class was even halfway finished.

■ Word scramble

1) OPULENT

2) VARIEGATED

3) INGENUITY

4) UNORTHODOX

5) HUMILITY

6) WRY

7) HAPHAZARDLY

8) WINSOME

9) NONCHALANT

10) THRONG

■ Matching

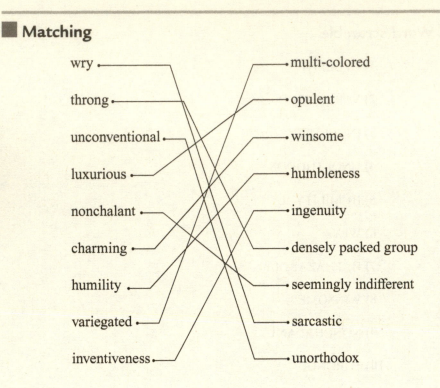

wry   multi-colored

throng   opulent

unconventional   winsome

luxurious   humbleness

nonchalant   ingenuity

charming   densely packed group

humility   seemingly indifferent

variegated   sarcastic

inventiveness   unorthodox

Review: Units 9 & 10

▌Grammar stretches

1. I saw Martina for a moment before she disappeared into the crowd that was ***thronging*** into the stadium.

2. Although he had been a professional football player, Mr. Smith spoke ***nonchalantly*** about that phase of his life and didn't seem to care whether or not other people knew of the details.

3. Given how many people in our society drink alcohol, it is impressive that you and your friends have chosen to ***abstain***.

4. The ***infamous*** nature of the Nazi regime is beyond dispute.

5. Because nobody knew what a difficult child Mr. Ingersoll's son had been, Ingersoll usually smiled ***wryly*** when he heard his son praised.

6. He was the first—and last—foot soldier to have had the ***audacity*** to request an audience with the king.

7. Gina was deeply impressed by the ***opulence*** of the Newport Mansions, homes to some of the richest people in America many years ago.

8. Stan's choice of clothing today was rather ***haphazard***, as he had only had five minutes to get ready in the morning.

9. After numerous affairs and other highly publicized sexual indiscretions, the actor's ***licentiousness*** had become common knowledge.

■ Error watch

1. Lynn's four-year-old son has an **_unorthodox_** method of getting dressed, as he puts his shoes and socks on before his pants.   Correct

2. The man's **_ingenuity_** can be seen in his many criminal convictions and other instances of bad behavior.   Incorrect

3. Mere knowledge is insufficient; only someone with great **_humility_** could be resourceful enough to solve this particular design problem. Incorrect

4. The way little Leanne screams when she gets frustrated is so **_winsome_**.   Incorrect

5. Before he was arrested, the killer's **_iniquity_** was the stuff of legend. Correct

Matching

humbleness	wickedness
sarcastic	abstained
licentious	luxurious
willingly refrained from	haphazardly
variegated	ingenuity
densely packed group	wry
seemingly indifferent	reputation for evil
charming	throng
infamy	nonchalant
iniquity	sexually immoral
opulent	humility
carelessly	fearless
unorthodox	winsome
inventiveness	unconventional
audacious	multi-colored

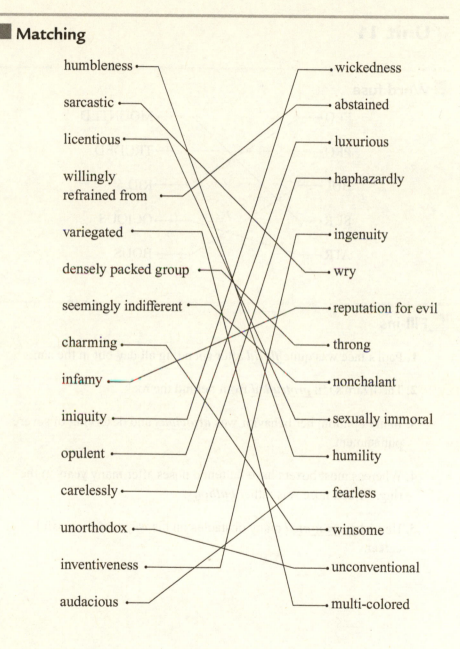

Unit 11

Word fuse

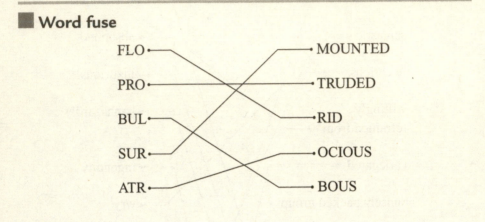

Fill-ins

1. Paul's face was quite **_florid_** after spending all day out in the sun.

2. The lizard's tail **_protruded_** from behind the rock.

3. In my opinion, her behavior was **_atrocious_** and deserving of severe punishment.

4. Whereas most boxers have flattened noses after many years in the ring, Mike's nose was rather **_bulbous_**.

5. He had **_surmounted_** many obstacles on his way to a successful career.

Word scramble

1) BULBOUS

2) SURMOUNTED

3) FLORID

4) ATROCIOUS

5) PROTRUDED

Matching

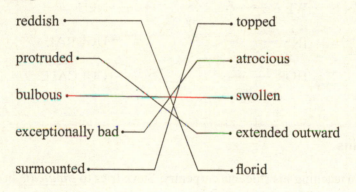

reddish ——— topped

protruded ——— atrocious

bulbous ——— swollen

exceptionally bad ——— extended outward

surmounted ——— florid

Unit 12

Word fuse

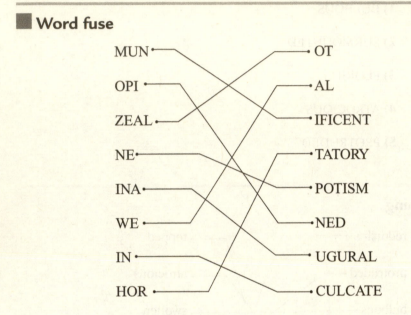

MUN   OT

OPI   AL

ZEAL   IFICENT

NE   TATORY

INA   POTISM

WE   NED

IN   UGURAL

HOR   CULCATE

Fill-ins

1. In teaching his students carpentry, Steve tries to ***inculcate*** in them respect for the materials and an appreciation of the craft.

2. My interest is not in protecting the wealthiest citizens, since they can take care of themselves, but rather in promoting the common ***weal***.

3. Even when his team was winning by a large margin, Coach Brown's halftime speeches were always strongly ***hortatory***.

4. Gifts from its most ***munificent*** citizens have allowed the town to remodel city hall.

5. Alice is a ***zealot*** about promoting clean energy whenever she can.

6. He planned to attend the ***inaugural*** ceremony marking the opening of his best friend's charter school.

7. "We need a new governor," ***opined*** Timothy, "and we need one now."

8. As his uncle is vice president of our company, it seems he got his job through ***nepotism*** rather than his own qualifications.

■ Word scramble

1) INCULCATE

2) OPINED

3) HORTATORY

4) INAUGURAL

5) ZEALOT

6) NEPOTISM

7) WEAL

8) MUNIFICENT

Matching

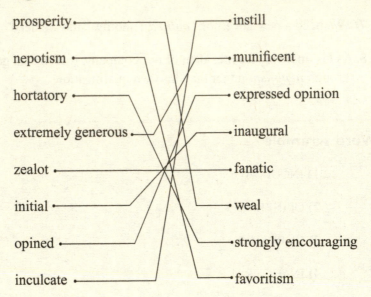

prosperity — instill

nepotism — munificent

hortatory — expressed opinion

extremely generous — inaugural

zealot — fanatic

initial — weal

opined — strongly encouraging

inculcate — favoritism

Review: Units 11 & 12

■ Grammar stretches

1. My daughter is not very good yet at playing hide-and-seek; whenever she hides behind something, some part of her is always ***protruding***.

2. The executive quite ***nepotistically*** awarded the summer internship to his niece.

3. The number of ***atrocities*** committed by their militia against ordinary citizens will never be fully revealed.

4. Although she had received an invitation, Patty was unable to attend the ***inauguration*** of the new governor.

5. If you try hard enough, you can ***surmount*** any obstacle.

6. Noriko is so ***zealous*** about cleanliness; she actually cleans her apartment two or three times a week!

7. The anonymous donor's ***munificence*** allowed the city to build a new park in the downtown area.

8. Because I don't know the facts of the Wilson case, I am unable to share with you my ***opinion*** as to his innocence.

9. The teacher did not appreciate the ***floridity*** of Jenn's wordy style.

■ Error watch

1. Jon listened to the complaint with a ***weal*** expression on his face.
Incorrect

2. I had thought that my mother's speech to me about the importance of finishing college would be threatening; instead, what she said turned out to be enthusiastic and ***hortatory***.   **Correct**

3. His forehead was not merely large; it was downright ***bulbous***.
Correct

4. Today is the one-month anniversary of Mykala's ***inculcation*** as president of our organization.   **Incorrect**

5. The criminal's gun ***surmounted*** from his coat pocket.   **Incorrect**

Matching

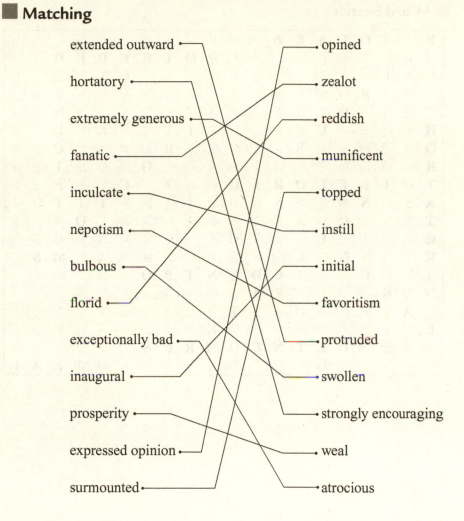

extended outward   • • opined

hortatory   • • zealot

extremely generous   • • reddish

fanatic   • • munificent

inculcate   • • topped

nepotism   • • instill

bulbous   • • initial

florid   • • favoritism

exceptionally bad   • • protruded

inaugural   • • swollen

prosperity   • • strongly encouraging

expressed opinion   • • weal

surmounted   • • atrocious

■ Word Search

```
B I T O L A E Z O O P N I C E E G R A S
M U L L E R L E S P R O T R U D E D U S
E A L E S T B A C T U S C I C T I D L H
N G I B H M P K E F V T A H V F N T S A
C R R F O Q R T I R A X T B S E N N T I
H E O E J U K E Z R P T T P O E K E W R
O A L W S A S P E O Y Y R C P Y O C S D
R I G D O T R U T L S O F O D Q N I A A
T O I E F L O R I D U B T E C U A F H N
A S O N E T A N N D N I T N A I T I U J
T A V I C H A Z T E S A L E R F O N T E
O R Y T F U N O I M T N E R M E B U O D
R T E W G O L O W P R O F B A W L M S G
Y E L U K T I C D E N I P O L G Y O P A
N U R Z O D T R A T O X S A L O A B H L
E A T L B X H A I T Y E I R O V I N U P
L R Y E C T H N C R E V T E C A W E N E
S A L E D E T N U O M R U S L S U P L E
C R I G A D E R P P O L E R R O W E A L
```

CHAPTER 3
Vocabulary Building: Crossword Puzzles

Overview

Each crossword puzzle in this chapter consists of words that are drawn from various units in Chapters 1 or 2. A small number of words is drawn from the contrasts or fast facts sections of unit reviews. Answers to the puzzles are given at the end of the chapter.

Crossword Puzzle #1

Chapter 1

Across

3. misstatement; lie
7. dangerous
8. impossible to attack
10. give someone essential information (also: a legal document)
12. well-reasoned
14. likely to
15. deeply involved
16. carefully
18. free from blame
19. not discouraged

Down

1. highly productive
2. behaving jocosely
4. soothe
5. long, angry speech
6. likely
9. become less
11. determined
13. sociable
17. freedom

Crossword Puzzle #2

Chapter 1

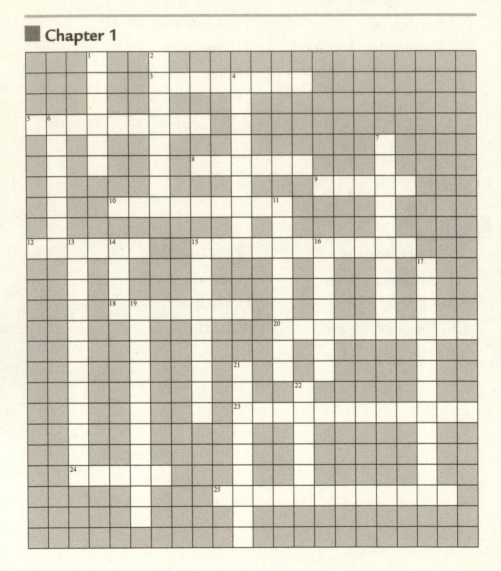

Across

3. about to happen
5. monetary
8. swamp
9. competing with
10. often complaining
12. pure

15. diligently
18. famous
20. ideal model
23. unwilling to compromise
24. representative works
25. unconventional behavior

Down

1. verbally attack
2. correct a mistaken belief
4. wicked
6. commemorative text
7. pacify
11. engaging in little physical activity
13. noble

14. scholarly book
15. difficulty
16. burdensome
17. punishment
19. generous and noble
21. playful
22. cowardly

Crossword Puzzle #3

Chapter 2

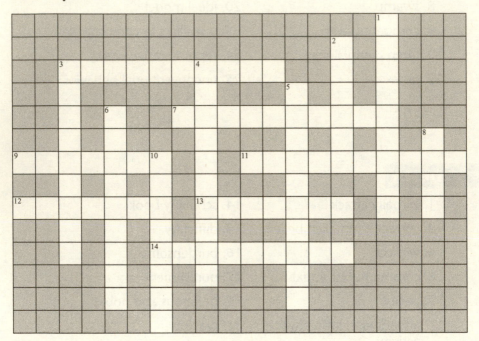

Across

3. independent
7. native
9. emotional distress
11. multi-colored

12. not yet decided
13. forced
14. persistent

Down

1. prevent
2. gloomy
3. willingly refrained from
4. extremely generous

5. stubborn
6. secretly
8. prosperity
10. trivial

Crossword Puzzle #4

Chapter 2

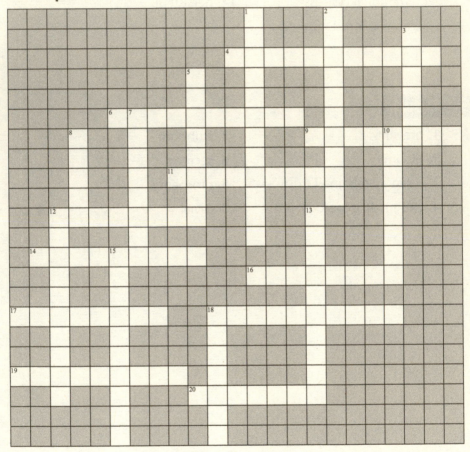

Across

4. lengthening
6. even-temperedness
9. beginner
11. hanging
12. irritable
14. pompous
16. clarity
17. threatening
18. seemingly indifferent
19. requested earnestly
20. not yet decided

Down

1. by chance
2. crosswise arrangement
3. reputation for evil
5. conscious
7. trivial complaints
8. cheat
10. humbleness
12. tendency
13. thinking again and again
15. excessively controlling
18. emerging

Crossword Puzzle #5

Chapters 1 & 2

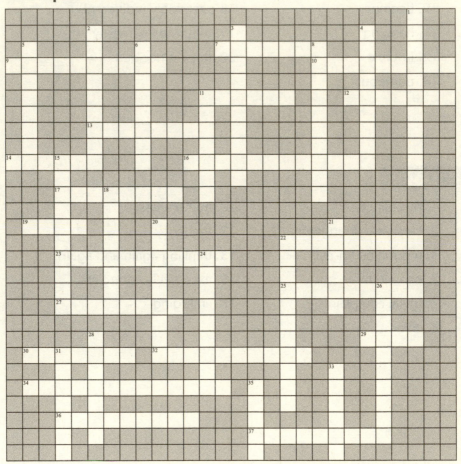

Across

7. foolish
9. without hope
10. not discouraged
11. disorderly mix
12. thwarted
13. not talkative
14. emotionless
16. set of names
17. traitor
19. provoke

22. exaggeration
23. anger over injustice
25. strongly encouraging
27. diminished
29. prosperity
30. awe-inspiring
32. insulting
34. gullibility
36. inventiveness
37. overly talkative

Down

1. overly dramatic and emotional behavior
2. deeply respected
3. shifted indecisively
4. easily managed
5. deeply respectful
6. formal tribute
8. topped
11. charming
15. talkative

18. false
20. spoke haltingly
21. scold angrily
24. intrusive
26. overly eager to please
28. reveal secret
31. conciseness of expression
33. ineffective
35. consider worthy

ANSWERS TO CROSSWORD PUZZLES

Crossword Puzzle #1

Chapter 1

				¹P									²J			
			³P	R	E	V	⁴A	R	I	C	A	⁵T	I	O	N	⁶I
				O			S					I	C			N
		⁷P	E	R	I	L	O	U	S			R	U			C
				I			⁸U	N	⁹A	S	S	A	I	L	A	B	L	E
	¹⁰B	¹¹R	I	E	F			A		B			D		A		I
		E		I				G		A			E		R		N
		S		¹²C	O	G	¹³E	N	T							E
¹⁴P	R	O	N	E			R			¹⁵E	M	B	R	O	I	L	E	D
	L						E									
	U			¹⁶G	I	N	G	E	R	¹⁷L	Y					
	T			A						I					
	¹⁸E	X	O	N	E	R	A	T	E		B					
				I						E					
				O						R					
				¹⁹U	N	D	A	U	N	T	E	D			
				S						Y					

Crossword Puzzle #2

Chapter 1

			[1] I			[2] D															
			M			[3] I	M	M	I	[4] N	E	N	T								
			P			S				E											
[5] P	[6] E	C	U	N	I	A	R	Y		F											
	P		G			B				A							[7] C				
	I		N			U		[8] M	O	R	A	S	S				O				
	T					S				I				[9] V	Y	I	N	G			
	A			[10] Q	U	E	R	U	L	O	U	[11] S					C				
	P									U		E					I				
[12] C	H	[13] A	S	[14] T	E			[15] A	S	S	I	D	U	[16] O	U	S	L	Y			
		R		O				D				E		N			I		[17] C		
		I		M				V				N		E			A		H		
		S		[18] E	[19] M	I	N	E	N	T		T		R			T		A		
		T			A			R				[20] A	P	O	T	H	E	O	S	I	S
		O			G			S				R		U					T		
		C			N			I		[21] W		Y		S					I		
		R			A			T		H			[22] C						S		
		A			N			Y		[23] I	N	T	R	A	N	S	I	G	E	N	T
		T			I					M			A						M		
		I			M					S			V						E		
		[24] C	A	N	O	N				I			E						N		
					U				[25] E	C	C	E	N	T	R	I	C	I	T	Y	
					S					A											
										L											

Crossword Puzzle #3

Chapter 2

```
                                        1F
                                   2M   O
      3A  U  T  O  N  O  4M  O  U  S      O    R
        B           U           5R        R    E
        S      6F  7I  N  D  I  G  E  N  O  U  S
        T      U   I              F         S   T        8W
  9C  H  A  G  R  I 10N      F  11V  A  R  I  E  G  A  T  E  D
        I      T   U   I            A           L      A
 12P  E  N  D  I  N  G     13C  O  E  R  C  E  D      L    L
        E      V   A   E              T
        D      E 14T  E  N  A  C  I  O  U  S
        L      O   T                 R
        Y      R   Y
               Y
```

Across: 3 AUTONOMOUS · 7 INDIGENOUS · 9 CHAGRIN · 11 VARIEGATED · 12 PENDING · 13 COERCED · 14 TENACIOUS

Down: 3 ABSTAINED · 6 FURTIVELY · 10 NUGATORY

Crossword Puzzle #4

Chapter 2

										¹F	O		²T	R				
										O			R			³I		
								⁴P	R	O	T	R	A	C	T	I	N	G
						⁵S			T	U		N	S			F		
						E			U			S	V			A		
				⁶E	Q	U	A	N	I	M	I	T	Y			M		
	⁸G		⁷U			T		T	O			⁹N	E	O	¹⁰P	H	Y	T	E
	O		I			I		T	O			R			U		
	U		B	¹¹P	E	N	D	U	L	O	U	S			M	I	
	G		B		N		S			E			I	
¹²P	E	T	U	L	A	N	T		L		¹³R			L	I	
R			E				Y		U			I	
¹⁴B	O	M	¹⁵B	A	S	T	I	C			M			T	
P		U					¹⁶L	U	C	I	D	I	T	Y	
E		T						N					
¹⁷M	I	N	A	T	O	R	Y		¹⁸N	O	N	C	H	A	L	A	N	T
S		C			A			T		
I		R			S			I		
¹⁹E	N	T	R	E	A	T	E	D	C			N		
Y		T			P	E	N	D	I	N	G		
		I			N				
		C			T				

Crossword Puzzle #5

Chapters 1 & 2

																				¹H
		²V					³V								⁴T		I			
⁵R		E		⁶E		⁷F	A	T	U	O	U	⁸S		R		S				
⁹D	E	S	P	O	N	D	E	N	T		C			¹⁰U	N	D	A	U	N	T	E	D
V		E		C			I			R		C		R			
E		R		O		¹¹W	E	L	T	E	R		M		¹²S	T	Y	M	I	E	D
R		A		M		I		L		M		A		O			
E		¹³T	A	C	I	T	U	R	N		A		T		U		B		N			
N		E		U		S		T		U		N		L		I			
¹⁴S	T	O	¹⁵L	I	D			¹⁶N	O	M	E	N	C	L	A	T	U	R	E			C	S
		O			M		D			E				S	
	¹⁷Q	U	I	¹⁸S	L	I	N	G		E				D	
	U		P										
¹⁹G	O	A	D		U		²⁰S				²¹B	
	C		R		T			²²H	Y	P	E	R	B	O	L	E	
²³I	N	D	I	G	N	A	T	I	²⁴O	N		A		R	
	O		O		M		F		A		A	
	U		U		M		F		²⁵H	O	R	T	A	T	²⁶O	R	Y	
²⁷S	U	B	S	I	D	E	D		I		A		E		B	
			R		C		A			S	
	²⁸D		E		I		A		²⁹W	E	A	L	
³⁰S	U	³¹B	L	I	M	E	³²D	E	R	O	G	A	T	O	R	Y		Q	
	R	V			U		D		³³F		U	
³⁴C	R	E	D	U	L	O	U	S	N	E	S	S	³⁵D	L		U		I	
	V	L			E		Y		T		O	
	³⁶I	N	G	E	N	U	I	T	Y		I		U	
	T	E			³⁷G	A	R	R	U	L	O	U	S	
	Y				N			E	

Overview

As you learn new words, it's important not to cram. Try to pace yourself. If you can, spend some time each day on vocabulary learning activities. In this chapter you will read about strategies that can help you learn advanced vocabulary.

Expanding Your Vocabulary Horizons

Reading

Read as much as you can. Try reading some genres (e.g., fiction, essays, journalism, etc.) that you are not used to reading. Use contextual clues to guess the meanings of unfamiliar words, then consult a dictionary to see whether you were correct. Keep a list of new words that you periodically review.

Writing and speaking

Whenever possible, use the words you're learning when you talk or write. Create sentences and even stories or essays with the words you learned in this book. For example, you learned that the word "hiatus" refers to a temporary break or gap. How could you use "hiatus" in a sentence? Could you write a brief story about someone who took a hiatus from work? In writing this story, can you make use of some of the other vocabulary you've learned? Did the person take a hiatus because he or she was despondent or morose about some recent adversity? Did the person vacillate about taking time off, or was he or she resolute about the plan?

Internet resources

Check the Internet for free vocabulary-building resources, including word-a-day sites, word game sites, and others.

Grammatical cues

Increase your awareness of how the constituents of words contribute to their meanings. Many English words are built from more basic constituents or building blocks that contribute to the meaning. These constituents may include prefixes, stems, and/or suffixes.

A stem can be thought of as part of a word that functions by itself as a word. For example, in the word "derailed," the stem is "rail."

A prefix is a part of a word added before the stem. For example, "de" is the prefix in "derailed."

A suffix is a part of a word added after the stem. In "derailed," the suffix is "ed." You can see from this example that if you had never heard the word "derailed" before, you would be able to guess what it means if you knew that one meaning of "de" is "off," that "rail" refers to the metal constituents of railroad tracks, and that as a suffix "ed" indicates past tense. Thus, in some cases, you can guess the meaning of an unfamiliar word by means of what you know about its constituents.

The following table contains some widely used prefixes. Along with each prefix you will see one of its meanings as well as two examples of words in which it appears. As time permits, you should familiarize yourself with these and other prefixes as well as suffixes, any of which may appear in GRE words.

Common Prefixes

Prefix	Meaning	Examples
a	not	*amoral* (not moral) *atypical* (not typical)
ante	before	*antecedent* (something that precedes something else) *antebellum* (before the war)
anti	against	*antipathy* (deep dislike) *antithesis* (counter-idea)
bene	good	*beneficial* (promoting well-being) *benevolent* (generous)
bi	two	*biannual* (twice per year) *biennial* (every two years)
bio	life	*biotic* (derived from living things) *biosphere* (part of planet where life occurs)

Common Prefixes

Prefix	Meaning	Examples
con	together	*conclave* (private meeting) *convene* (gather together)
contra	against	*contradict* (assert the opposite) *contraindicated* (inadvisable)
de	remove	*decontaminate* (eliminate germs) *defoliate* (remove leaves)
dis	not	*disaffected* (resentful) *discontent* (not content)
dys	bad	*dysfunctional* (functioning poorly) *dyspeptic* (having indigestion; irritable)
equi	equal	*equidistant* (at equal distances) *equilateral* (having all sides equal)
ex	out	*excavate* (dig out) *extract* (pull out)
hyper	over	*hyperactive* (overly active) *hypertension* (high blood pressure)
hypo	under	*hypodermic* (under the skin) *hypotension* (low blood pressure)
inter	between	*internecine* (involving conflict within a group) *interpersonal* (between people)
intra	within	*intramural* (within school) *intrapersonal* (within a person)
mono	single	*monochromatic* (one color) *monotone* (unvarying in tone)
multi	many	*multichromatic* (involving more than one color) *multifaceted* (having many facets)

Common Prefixes

Prefix	Meaning	Examples
ortho	straight	*orthodox* (strictly conventional) *orthogonal* (at right angles)
pan	all	*panacea* (cure-all) *pantheon* (temple for all gods)
poly	many	*polygamy* (marriage with more than two partners) *polysyllabic* (having multiple syllables)
post	after	*postgraduate* (after graduation) *postpartum* (after birth)
pre	before	*precede* (go before) *prenuptial* (before marriage)
pro	for	*proclivity* (tendency) *proponent* (supporter)
pseudo	false	*pseudonym* (false name) *pseudoscience* (false science)
re	again	*recidivism* (relapse to undesirable behavior) *revamp* (renovate)
sub	under	*submit* (yield to) *substandard* (inferior in quality)
super	over	*supercilious* (looking down on) *supersede* (take over)
ultra	beyond	*ultraconservative* (extremely conservative) *ultrasonic* (above the speed of sound)
un	not	*unreliable* (not reliable) *untested* (not tested)

Overview

In this chapter you will learn about the types of questions that appear in the GRE Verbal Reasoning section.

Verbal Reasoning at a Glance

The GRE revised General Test, which was launched in August 2011, differs in several ways from the old version of the test. Most notably, new types of questions are used. The computer-based (ETS calls this "computer adaptive") format is more flexible and user-friendly. And there are differences in cost, in the timing of score reporting, and in the scale used to report the scores. All of these changes are intended to make the test experience better for you. The ETS website gives more information about what's new in the GRE revised General Test: *http://www.ets.org/gre/revised_general/know.*

The Verbal Reasoning section of the GRE revised General Test contains new types of questions. At the same time, the antonyms and analogies have been dropped from this section. The result is that there are now no questions that test vocabulary out of context.

According to ETS, the new Verbal Reasoning section tests higher-order cognitive abilities such as the ability to understand multiple levels of meaning, to summarize what you read, and to understand the meanings of words and sentences. Specifically, you will find three types of questions in the Verbal Reasoning section: Reading Comprehension, Text Completion, and Sentence Equivalence. Below you will find a description of each question type, and then an example question corresponding to each.

Examples of Question Types

Reading comprehension

Reading Comprehension questions are presented in sets. Each set of questions pertains to a passage; in all, you will be reading about 10 passages.

Most of the passages will consist of a single paragraph, although a few will range from three to five paragraphs. The content of the passages is drawn from a variety of academic and non-academic sources. You will find three types of questions:

1. "Multiple-choice Questions" consist of a question followed by five options. In order to receive credit, you must choose the correct option.

2. "Multiple-choice Questions—Select One or More Answer Choices" consist of a question followed by three options. You may select one, two, or three options as your answer. In order to receive credit, you must choose all and only the correct options. In other words, no partial credit is given.

3. "Select-in-Passage" questions ask you to click on the sentence in a passage that fits a certain description.

    To illustrate each type of Reading Comprehension question, consider the following passage:

The development of the arts in Russia was profoundly influenced by Catherine II, who ruled the country from 1762 through 1796. A prominent example is the creation of the State Hermitage (known familiarly as "the Hermitage"), one of the largest museums of art and culture in the world. The Hermitage began as Catherine's private collection, acquired over a period of three decades from prominent sources throughout Europe. Catherine was a brilliant, enlightened ruler with a deep appreciation for the art and artists she supported. By the time of her death, the collection consisted of more than 70,000 books, paintings, and other cultural artifacts. Although the Hermitage was not open to the public until 1852, more than a half century after Catherine's passing, her patronage was the foundation of this international treasure.

Example of multiple-choice question

The passage is primarily concerned with which of the following?

    (A) Catherine II's influence on the development of the arts in Europe

    (B) Interrelationships between power, money, and culture

    (C) The connection between Catherine II and the State Hermitage

    (D) Historical influences on the creation of national museums

    Correct answer: **C**

Example of multiple-choice question—select one or more answer choices

Consider each of the following choices separately and select all that apply. The passage implies which of the following?

    [A] Catherine's influence on the arts in Russia was not limited to her private collections.

    [B] Catherine never had any intention of opening her collections to the Russian public.

    [C] Catherine's patronage was motivated at least in part by a deep appreciation for art.

    Correct answer: **A** and **C**

Example of select-in-passage question

Select the sentence that most concretely demonstrates the extent of Catherine's patronage.

Correct Answer: **"By the time of her death, the collection consisted of more than 70,000 books, paintings, and other cultural artifacts."**

Text completion

Text Completion questions consist of passages ranging in length from one to five sentences. Each passage contains one to three blanks. You are asked to choose a word or words that best fill in the blank(s). For a passage that contains one blank, you will choose from among five words to fill in the blank. For passages that contain two or three blanks, you will choose from among three words to fill in each blank. No partial credit is given.

Example of text-completion question

Directions: For each blank select one entry from the corresponding column of choices. Fill all blanks in the way that best completes the text.

A government advisory panel recently concluded that artificial colorings in food do not cause hyperactivity in children; thus, parents need not (i) _____ about their children consuming foods that contain these chemicals, and there is no need for foods that contain artificial colorings to have (ii) _____ labels.

Blank (i)	Blank (ii)
Ⓐ rejoice	Ⓓ warning
Ⓑ worry	Ⓔ nutritional
Ⓒ reminisce	Ⓕ attractive

Correct answer: **B** and **D**

Sentence equivalence

Sentence equivalence questions consist of a single sentence that contains a blank. You are asked to choose two words out of a set of six that best fill in the blank. Each word you choose should fit the meaning of the sentence as a whole and result in sentences that are comparable in meaning. Again, no partial credit is given.

Example of sentence-equivalence question

Directions: Select the *two* answer choices that, when used to complete the sentence, fit the meaning of the sentence as a whole *and* produce completed sentences that are alike in meaning.

The teacher was startled by the hostile tone of the student's question, because this particular student had always seemed to have an especially _____ temperament.

A uncooperative
B aggressive
C meek
D wary
E mild
F dismissive

Correct Answer: **C** and **E**

CHAPTER
GRE Verbal Reasoning: Strategies for Success

Overview

This chapter provides an introduction to strategies for success on the Verbal Reasoning section of the GRE revised General Test.

General Strategies

Now that you've mastered the vocabulary in this book and are continuing to learn on your own, what else can you do to boost your performance on the Verbal Reasoning section?

First, here is some general advice about preparing for the test.

1. Make use of the free test preparation materials that ETS provides to anyone who registers for the GRE revised General Test. (See *http://www.ets.org/gre/revised_general/prepare*.) Have a look at these materials, as they provide helpful information and examples about all sections of the test, including Verbal Reasoning.

2. Take a look at the ETS web pages devoted to the Verbal Reasoning section (see *http://www.ets.org/gre/revised_general/know*). Here too you will find useful information and examples.

3. Do some planning for the days leading up to the test. Avoid last-minute cramming, as that can be counterproductive. Try to get sufficient rest the night before the test, and allow enough travel time so that you don't have to rush to get to the testing site.

4. Plan carefully for test day. It is especially important to consult your registration materials and the ETS website for information about what you should and should not bring to the test (see *http://www.ets.org/gre/revised_general/test_day*). For example, you will need to bring valid identification, as defined by ETS. If you are taking the paper-based version of the test, you will need to bring three or four sharpened pencils (No. 2 or HB) and an eraser. However, regardless of whether you take the paper-based or computer-based version, you will <u>not</u> be allowed to bring into the test center any of the following:

   (a) Electronic or photographic devices

   (b) Food, beverages, or tobacco

(c) Personal items other than identification documents

(d) Scratch paper (the center will provide you with scratch paper).

5. Familiarize yourself with the different types of questions you will see in each section of the test, including Verbal Reasoning. (See Chapter 5 for a discussion of question types in this section.)

Second, here are some suggestions that are specific to each type of question in the Verbal Reasoning section:

Reading-comprehension Strategies

1. Reading Comprehension questions will represent many different disciplines, and so you should expect to encounter topics with which you have little or no familiarity. Keep in mind that all of the information you will need to answer the questions are contained in the passages.

2. You should read each passage first before answering the questions, although in some cases glancing at the questions may provide some guidance. As you read each passage, try to

   (a) identify the theme or main idea, and consider how details are used to support that idea.

   (b) make note of the relationships between different ideas expressed in the passage—are they consistent or contrasting, overlapping or separate, etc.

   (c) be aware of the author's purpose—is he or she reporting facts, developing a theory, engaging in speculation, or attempting to persuade?

   (d) make note of whether the author is neutral or committed to a particular opinion or perspective.

To illustrate these suggestions, consider again this sample passage from Chapter 5:

> The development of the arts in Russia was profoundly influenced by Catherine II, who ruled the country from 1762 through 1796. A prominent example is the creation of the State Hermitage (known familiarly as "the Hermitage"), one of the largest museums of art and culture in the world. The Hermitage began as Catherine's private collection, acquired over a period of three decades from prominent sources throughout Europe. Catherine was a brilliant, enlightened ruler with a deep appreciation for the art and artists she supported. By the time of her death, the collection consisted of more than 70,000 books, paintings, and other cultural artifacts. Although the Hermitage was not open to the public until 1852, more than a half century after Catherine's passing, her patronage was the foundation of this international treasure.

If you were reading this passage during the test, you should note that the author's purpose seems to be to relate a set of historical facts. You should note that the author's approach is generally neutral, although phrases such as "profoundly influenced, "brilliant, enlightened ruler. . . ." and "international treasure" suggests that the author has a very positive view of Catherine and the State Hermitage. And you should note that entire discussion of the Hermitage is intended to illustrate the idea expressed in the opening sentence, while most of the details serve to clarify Catherine's role in the creation of this museum.

3. After finishing the passage, read each question carefully. Answer the questions solely on the basis of information given in the passage. Do not make use of background knowledge or personal opinion when answering the questions.

Text-completion Strategies

1. Like Reading Comprehension passages, Text Completion passages will reflect a variety of topics. Whether you are familiar or unfamil-

iar with a particular topic, you should restrict your attention to the information in the passage, as you will not need to make use of other information to answer the question. And you should read the passage first before answering the questions.

2. In the interest of accuracy and time, avoid considering each possible combination of answers. Rather, consider what seems to fit the blanks in a way that is sensible, and then check to see whether similar words are given among the answer choices.

3. Identify words that seem especially important, because they are critical to an understanding of the sentence, and/or because they tell you something about the logic of the sentence (e.g., words such as "therefore" or "moreover").

4. If there is more than one blank, you may or may not want to focus on the first blank, as it may or may not be the easiest to fill.

5. Once you have made your selection(s), go back to see whether the sentence is sensible as well as logically, grammatically, and stylistically coherent.

To illustrate these suggestions, consider again this sample Text Completion question from Chapter 5:

For each blank select one entry from the corresponding column of choices. Fill all blanks in the way that best completes the text.

A government advisory panel recently concluded that artificial colorings in food do not cause hyperactivity in children; thus, parents need not (i) _____ about their children consuming foods that contain these chemicals, and there is no need for foods that contain artificial colorings to have (ii) _____ labels.

Blank (i)	Blank (ii)
Ⓐ rejoice	Ⓓ warning
Ⓑ worry	Ⓔ nutritional
Ⓒ reminisce	Ⓕ attractive

The first clause of the sentence asserts that according to an expert panel, artificial colorings in food do not have a particular adverse effect. You may or may not agree with this assertion, but this is the information that you should work with in selecting your answers. The word "thus" is a critical word, because it indicates that the remainder of the sentence draws out the logical implications of the panel's findings; you should also see that each "need not" corresponds to one of those implications. In short, the remainder of the sentence describes what need <u>not</u> happen as a result of the findings of the expert panel. Logically, what need not happen as a result of their findings is fear or concern over the presence of artificial colorings in food. This is what you should have in mind as you read the passage. Thus, even before you see the answer options, you should guess that the first blank should be filled by a word such as "worry," while the second blank should be filled by a word such as "warning." Options B and D are the only ones that are sensible and consistent with the meaning of the sentence (although all of the options are grammatically appropriate).

Sentence-equivalence Strategies

1. Read the entire sentence in order to get an overall sense of the meaning.

2. Pay particular attention to words that indicate the structure or logic of the sentence (e.g., words such as "therefore" or "moreover").

3. As you read, think of a word that seems to fill in the blank, and then see if two similar words are given among the answer choices.

4. One you have chosen two words, make sure that inserting each one results in a sentence that is sensible, as well as logically, grammatically, and stylistically coherent. You will also need to make sure that the two sentences have the same meaning.

To illustrate these suggestions, consider again this sample Sentence Equivalence question from Chapter 5:

Select the *two* answer choices that, when used to complete the sentence, fit the meaning of the sentence as a whole *and* produce completed sentences that are alike in meaning.

The teacher was startled by the hostile tone of the student's question, because this particular student had always seemed to have an especially _____ temperament.

A uncooperative
B aggressive
C meek
D wary
E mild
F dismissive

As you read this sentence, you should see that the word "because" is critical, as it tells you that the second clause of the sentence explains why the teacher was startled. As you read through the second clause, you should expect the blank to be most suitably filled by some word that is opposite in meaning to "hostile." You may not be thinking specifically of "meek" and "mild" (the two correct answers), but you should have words like this in mind. Thus, when you see the answer options, you will be able to rule out options A, B, D, and F immediately. And, when you imagine two sentences in which "meek" and "mild" are inserted in the blank, you will see that each sentence is logically, grammatically, and stylistically coherent, and that the two sentences have the same meaning.

INDEX OF KEY GRE TERMS

A

Abate, 6
Abstained, 191
Adversity, 3
Advocate, 135
Alleviate, 28, 35
Apotheosis, 6
Append, 158
Aristocratic, 74
Assiduously, 59, 63
Assuage, 6, 35, 157
Atrocious, 204
Audacious, 191
Autocratic, 177
Autonomous, 148
Awry, 199

B

Berate, 15, 22, 77
Besotted, 32
Bombastic, 135, 143
Brevity, 135, 143
Brief, 143
Brimming, 139
Bulbous, 204

C

Canon, 74, 78
Chagrin, 163
Chaste, 49
Chastened, 49
Chastisement, 45, 49

Coerced, 177
Cogent, 54
Cognizant, 166, 171, 185
Conciliate, 3, 10, 35
Consonant, 10
Consummate, 54, 62–63
Counterpart, 45
Craven, 68
Credulousness, 54

D

Deign, 35
Derogatory, 15
Descry, 6, 10
Despondent, 166
Disabuse, 54
Discern, 19
Disconcerting, 139
Dissemble, 54, 62
Divulged, 166

E

Eccentricity, 45
Embroiled, 15
Eminent, 3, 10
Encomium, 68
Ensued, 139
Entails, 166
Entreated, 181
Epitaph, 32
Equanimity, 148
Exhortatory, 211
Exonerate, 68

F

Fatuous, 152, 157
Fervid, 54
Florid, 204, 211
Forestall, 152
Fortuitously, 139
Furtively, 163
Futile, 28

G

Garrulous, 28, 62
Gaudy, 181
Gauge, 157
Gingerly, 6
Goad, 166
Gouge, 152, 157
Gregarious, 28

H

Haphazardly, 195
Hereditary, 45
Heterodoxy, 199
Hiatus, 181
Histrionics, 181
Hortatory, 207, 211
Humility, 195
Hyperbole, 135

I

Imminent, 3, 10
Immune, 211
Impugn, 15, 22, 77
Inaugural, 207
Incisively, 19
Inclined, 45, 49

Inconspicuous, 181
Inculcate, 207
Indigenous, 181
Indignation, 32, 35
Inept, 59
Infamy, 191
Ingenious, 199
Ingenuity, 195, 199
Iniquity, 191
Innate, 185
Insensible, 6
Intransigent, 15, 22

J

Jocosely, 45, 49
Jocular, 49
Jovially, 6, 49

L

Lacerate, 32
Libertine, 36
Liberty, 32, 35–36
Licentious, 191
Loquacious, 54, 62
Lucidity, 152
Ludicrous, 152, 157

M

Magnanimous, 68, 77
Magnate, 77
Minatory, 152, 157
Mollify, 148, 157
Morass, 19, 143
Morose, 139, 143
Munificent, 207, 211

N

Nascent, 181, 185
Natal, 185
Nefarious, 68
Neophyte, 139
Nepotism, 207
Nomenclature, 181
Nonchalant, 195
Nugatory, 139

O

Oblivious, 181
Obsequious, 68
Obstreperous, 139
Obviate, 152
Officious, 139, 143
Onerous, 59
Opined, 207
Opulent, 195

P

Pageant, 177
Pecuniary, 41
Pendant, 157–158
Pending, 158
Pendulous, 157–158
Perilous, 28
Petulant, 148
Preclude, 15
Prevarication, 54, 62
Proclaimed, 166
Prolific, 74
Pronation, 23
Prone, 19, 23, 49
Propensity, 148, 157–158
Protracting, 163

Protruded, 204
Pugilist, 22
Pugnacious, 22

Q

Querulous, 28
Quibbles, 152
Quisling, 68

R

Reconnaissance, 171
Reconnoiter, 171
Refractory, 152
Rejoinder, 15
Remunerate, 211
Resilient, 166
Resolute, 19, 22, 62, 185
Reverberate, 3
Reverent, 45
Ruminating, 139

S

Saturate, 28
Sedentary, 63
Sediment, 63
Sedulous, 63
Sentient, 177, 185
Soporific, 41
Spurious, 54
Stammered, 163
Stolidity, 41
Stymied, 166
Sublime, 177
Subsided, 152
Surmounted, 204, 211

T

Taciturn, 28
Tenacious, 181, 185
Throng, 195
Tirade, 15
Tome, 74
Torpor, 41
Tractable, 148
Transgressions, 68
Transverse, 185
Traversing, 181, 185

U

Unabated, 74
Unassailable, 59
Unassuming, 135, 143
Undaunted, 59, 62
Unorthodox, 195, 199

V

Vacated, 163, 171
Vacillated, 166
Vacuous, 171

Variegated, 195
Venerated, 74
Vicariously, 166
Vilified, 68, 77
Vying, 6

W

Weal, 207, 211
Welter, 166
Whimsical, 41
Winsome, 195
Wry, 195, 199

Z

Zeal, 211
Zealot, 207